GOD'S WORD
FOR A JR. HIGH WO

Teens of the Bible

Gospel Light

Dave & Kim Zovak, Author
Kara Eckmann Powell, General Editor

Gospel Light is an evangelical Christian publisher dedicated to serving the local church. We believe God's vision for Gospel Light is to provide church leaders with biblical, user-friendly materials that will help them evangelize, disciple and minister to children, youth and families.

We hope this Gospel Light resource will help you discover biblical truth for your own life and help you minister to youth. God bless you in your work.

For a free catalog of resources from Gospel Light please contact your Christian supplier or contact us at 1-800-4-GOSPEL.

PUBLISHING STAFF
William T. Greig, Publisher
Dr. Elmer L. Towns, Senior Consulting Publisher
Dr. Gary S. Greig, Senior Consulting Editor
Pam Weston, Editor
Patti Pennington Virtue, Assistant Editor
Christi Goeser, Editorial Assistant
Kyle Duncan, Associate Publisher
Bayard Taylor, M.Div., Senior Editor, Theological and Biblical Issues
Kevin Parks, Cover Designer
Debi Thayer, Designer
Duffy Robbins, Natalie Chenault and Siv Ricketts, Contributing Writers
ISBN 0-8307-2412-5
© 2000 by Gospel Light
All rights reserved.
Printed in U.S.A.

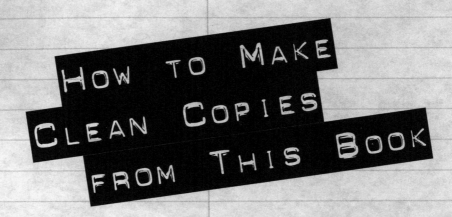

How to Make Clean Copies from This Book

You may make copies of portions of this book with a clean conscience if:

- you (or someone in your organization) are the original purchaser;
- you are using the copies you make for a noncommercial purpose (such as teaching or promoting your ministry) within your church or organization;
- you follow the instructions provided in this book.

However, it is ILLEGAL for you to make copies if:

- you are using the material to promote, advertise or sell a product or service other than for ministry fund-raising;
- you are using the material in or on a product for sale;
- you or your organization are **not** the original purchaser of this book.

By following these guidelines you help us keep our products affordable.

Thank you,

Gospel Light

As a professor and trainer of youth ministers, this is the best concept for junior high discipleship that I have ever seen. I love this curriculum not only because it gets Scripture into the hands and hearts of junior highers, but it does it in a way that they can grab hold of and enjoy. There is none better than Kara Eckmann Powell to ensure the integrity, depth and appropriateness of this tool. The **Pulse** curriculum is going to be a landmark resource for years to come. —**Chapman R. Clark, Ph.D.,** Associate Professor of Youth and Family Ministry, Fuller Theological Seminary

What I really appreciate about the **Pulse** series is that it fleshes out what I consider to be two absolute essentials for great curriculum: biblical depth and active learning. It is obvious that this is a curriculum designed by youth workers who care about junior high kids and who deeply care about helping them grow in their walk with Jesus. —**Duffy Robbins,** Associate Professor, Department of Youth Ministry, Eastern College

The youth leader's biggest challenge today is to relevantly translate the gospel to this generation. Kara has written a game plan for doing just that! **Pulse** is a curriculum that will help God's Word to become real for your students and will help you to reach a diverse generation—from the edgy/techno savvy to the more conservative student. It will produce a life change in (you)th! —**Larry Acosta,** President, The Hispanic Ministry Center

Pulse will help youth leaders create a great learning environment, provide a solid biblical education and challenge students to practice their faith daily. If leaders will use the variety of learning activities and creative teaching ideas, they will bring excellence to every lesson while enjoying the benefit of a simplified preparation time. —**Lynn Ziegenfuss,** Vice President of People Development, Youth for Christ/USA

In a world where Truth has been hidden in tolerance and where God has become the god of one's choice, Truth and solid biblical principles must be imparted to our students. **Pulse** CAPITALIZES both God and Truth. It's real, it's relevant, and it's *the* Truth! —**Monty L. Hipp,** Youth Communicator, Creative Communications

This is the best junior high/middle school curriculum to come out in years. Students will love this curriculum. —**Jim Burns, Ph.D.,** President, YouthBuilders

Wow! I'm impressed with the quality and the message this curriculum brings to millennials. It's going to be fun to use this material with kids! —**Charles Kim,** *JDM—Journey Devotional Magazine*, The Oriental Mission Church

Kara knows students, teaching, youth workers and the Bible; and she mixes that with a passion for God's Word. It seems that everything Kara touches is gold and I believe this **Pulse** curriculum not only bears her name, but her touch as well. Thanks, Kara, for another great contribution to youth ministry. —**Doug Fields,** Youth Pastor of Saddleback Church and author of *Purpose Driven Youth Ministry*

Pulse
Teens of the Bible

CONTENTSCONTENTSCONTENTSCONTENTSCONTENTS

Unit I: Outrageous Old Testament Teens

Unit II: Notable New Testament Teens

Dedication

This curriculum is dedicated to all youth leaders who make a Christ-centered impression on the lives of young people.

Dave and Kim

I also want to dedicate this book to those who helped me encounter God during my youth. I am especially grateful for those like Dennis and Sarah Mann and Wendell and Marie Conover who modeled following Jesus and invited me to do the same.

Kim

In particular, I thank Rev. Scott Erdman, Steve Norris, Dick Loftus, Debbie Williamson and the various staff members at Forest Home Christian Conference Center, California, for directing my junior high life toward Jesus and for putting up with all my obnoxious deeds.

Dave

....You've Made the Right Choice in Choosing Pulse for Your Junior Highers

The Top Ten Reasons...

9. Junior highers need and deserve youth workers who are expert trainers and teachers of biblical truth.

Every book is pulsating with youth leader tips and a full-length youth worker article designed to infuse YOU with more passion and skill for your ministry to junior highers.

10. Junior highers equate who God is with what church is like. To them a boring youth ministry means a boring God.

Fun and variety are the twin threads that weave their way through this curriculum's every page.

8. Junior highers need ongoing reminders of the big idea of each session.

Wouldn't it be great if you could give your students devotionals every week to reinforce the learning goals of the session? Get this: YOU CAN because THIS CURRICULUM DOES.

7. Some of our world's most effective evangelists are junior highers.

Every session, and we mean EVERY session, concludes with an evangelism option that ties "the big idea" of the session to the big need to share Christ with others.

6. Since no two junior highers (or their leaders) look, think or act alike, no two junior high ministries look, think or act alike.

Each step comes with three options that you can cut and paste to create a session that works best for YOUR students and YOUR personality.

5. Junior highers' growing minds are ready for more than just fun and games with a little Scripture thrown in.

Scripture is the very skeleton of each session, giving it its shape, its form and its very life.

4. Junior highers learn best when they can see, taste, feel and experience the session.

This curriculum involves students in every step through active learning and games to prove to students that following Christ is the greatest adventure ever.

3. Tragically, most junior highers are under challenged in their walks with Christ.

We've packed the final step of each session with three options that serve to move students a few steps forward in their walks with Christ.

2. Junior highers tend to understand the Bible in bits and pieces and miss the big picture of all that God has done for them.

This curriculum follows a strategic three-year plan that walks junior highers through the Bible, stopping at the most important points along the way.

1. Junior highers are moving through all sorts of changes—from getting a new body to getting a new locker.

We've designed a curriculum that revolves around one simple vision: moving God's Word into a junior high world.

Moving Through Pulse

Since **Pulse** is vibrating with so many different learning activities, this guide will help you pick and choose the best possible options for *your* students.

THE SESSIONS

The six sessions are split into two stand-alone units, so you can choose to teach either three or six sessions at a time. Each session is geared to be 45 to 90 minutes long and is comprised of the following four steps.

IT'S YOUR MOVE

A training article for you, the youth worker, to show you *why* and *how* to see students' worlds changed by Christ to change the world.

STEP 1 — MOVING IN

This first step helps students focus in on the theme of the lesson in a fun and engaging way through three options:

 MOVE IT—An active learning experience that may or may not involve all of your students.

 CHAT ROOM—Provocative, clear and simple questions to get your students thinking and chatting.

 FUN AND GAMES—Zany, creative and competitive games that may or may not involve all of your students.

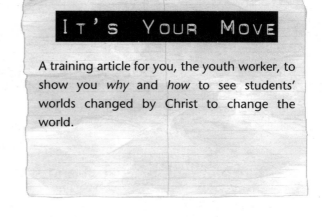

STEP 2 — MOVING UP

The second step enables students to look up to God by relating the very words of Scripture to the session topic through three options:

 MOVE IT—An active learning experience that may or may not involve all of your students.

 CHAT ROOM—Provocative, clear and simple questions to get your students chatting about the Scripture lesson.

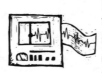 **PULSE POINTS**—A message outline with simple points and meaningful illustrations to give students some massive truths about Scripture with hardly any preparation on your part.

STEP 3

MOVING ON

STEP 4

MOVING OUT

This step asks students to look inward and discover how God's Word connects with their own worlds through three options:

 CHAT ROOM—Provocative, clear and simple questions to get your students chatting.

 REAL LIFE—A case study about someone (usually a junior higher) who needs your students' help figuring out what to do.

 TOUGH QUESTIONS—Four to six mind-stretching questions that challenge students to a new level of depth and integration.

This final step leads students out into their world with specific challenges to apply at school, at home and with their friends through three options based on your students' growth potential:

 LIGHT THE FIRE—For junior highers who may or may not be Christians and need easily accessible application ideas.

 FIRED UP—For students who are definitely Christians and are ready for more intense application ideas.

 SPREAD THE FIRE—A special evangelism application idea for students with a passion to see others come to know Christ.

OTHER IMPORTANT MOVING PARTS

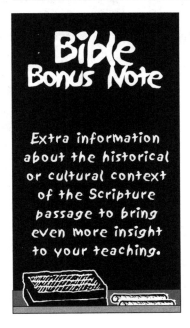

Bible Bonus Note

Extra information about the historical or cultural context of the Scripture passage to bring even more insight to your teaching.

Youth Leader Tip

Suggestions, options and/or other useful information to make your life easier or at least more interesting!

Devotions in Motion

WEEK FIVE: GRACE

Four devoTionals for each session To keep The big idea moving Through your junior highers' lives all week long.

ON THE MOVE—An appealing, easy-to-read handout you can give your junior highers to make sure they learn how to Christianity differs from other religions.

Contributors

Duffy Robbins chairs the youth ministry department at Eastern College in St. Davids, Pennsylvania. A member of the Youth Specialties National Resource Seminar team and a popular speaker at teen and youth leader conferences, Duffy is the author of *The Ministry of Nurture* and coauthor of *Spontaneous Melodramas* and *Memory Makers*.

Natalie Chenault, author of the student devotionals, enjoys diet soda and pudding cups. She attends Eastern College and loves hanging out with junior highers. She hopes to appear on *Jeopardy!* one day.

Siv Ricketts, author of the student article "What Is Really Different About Christianity?" is a student ministries director, freelance writer and editor living in San Diego, California. Siv and her husband, Dave, have been ministering to students together for the past six years and have recently been blessed with a new son, Corban.

Talking 'Bout My Generation: Using Young Lives to Touch Young Lives

Nothing fascinates kids like watching other kids. If you don't believe it, watch MTV's "Real World" or "Road Rules" one week and note the candid conversations, the outbursts, the complex moral dilemmas and the shaky camera shots that give the feeling of spontaneity and a first-person viewpoint. Teenagers watch these shows with the same loyalty that their grandparents followed Lucy and Ricky Ricardo. It may not be literary genius, but it works with teenagers—and it works big time!

THE REAL WORD AND GOD'S RULES

Real life—or even something that just appears to be real life—can grab a junior higher's attention like almost nothing else can. That's why this series of Bible studies on the lives of young people can be such a strategic tool for teaching your students. It gives them a chance to see real-life people facing real-life issues in the hands of a real-life God. These teens of the Bible give your junior highers a great chance to see how the real-life Word of God intersects with their real-life worlds for many reasons.

Kids want a hero.

Whether it's Michael Jordan, Dennis Rodman, Marilyn Manson or Yoda, kids seem to be drawn to someone they can gain a sense of identity from. Exposing your students to the stories of young people like the daring Daniel, who was willing to risk his life to be faithful to his God, or the teenage mother

It's Your Move

Mary, who in a combination of miracle and scandal finds herself unmarried, pregnant yet faithful to God, gives your students a chance to meet the kind of heroes that don't get much press in pop culture.

Kids learn best from other kids.

There seems to be something especially compelling to teenagers who hear about or witness one of their peers living out his or her faith in God. It's part of what made the story of the young martyrs at the 1999 Columbine High School shooting so powerful for students. They heard some of their own in perhaps the most difficult situation say "Yes, I believe in Jesus." In this series of studies the focus is not on 75-year-old Abraham, 300-year-old Enoch or 969-year-old Methuselah. The focus is on young people and their experiences with God.

Kids would rather hear a story with a moral than a lecture about morality.

William Kilpatrick, in his book *Why Johnny Can't Tell Right from Wrong*, argues that one of the reasons moral education has taken such a nosedive in this culture is because we have forgotten the power of good stories told well.

When I was a little boy, my parents always warned me about venturing out too far into the ocean. There might be a riptide, an undertow or any number of dangers lurking. But, of course, I completely disregarded their advice. I knew the ocean as nothing more than a vast, watery playground inhabited by animals like Flipper and Shamu. At least, that was what I thought until I saw the movie *Jaws*. From that day forth everything changed! It used to be "Last one in is a rotten egg"; now it was "Mom, why don't you and Dad go in first?" Almost overnight my attitudes about the ocean shifted dramatically. Why? Because I had been given a very vivid account of what could happen in that watery playground—and I didn't want to play anymore.

Such is the power of stories—even though I knew that this wasn't a true one! A good story told well can shape us and mold our perceptions in profound ways. No wonder Jesus never began his teaching with the words, "My topic for today is forgiveness." Instead it was "There was a man who had two sons." Once upon eternity.

Kids respond to realness.

Have fun with these studies. Don't try to sanitize the gritty details of these biblical teens who, although virtuous, also had real-life flaws and sins. Don't sacrifice the telling of the story so that you can hammer home the moral. Just let God speak through His Word. These stories that you will be studying have been shaping the faith and the history of people since the beginning of time. Enjoy this opportunity to give your junior highers a taste of the *real Word*!

Duffy Robbins
Chairman, Youth Ministries
Eastern College

The Big Idea

Learning to recognize and obey God's voice helps you to hear from Him.

Session Aims

In this session you will guide students to:

- Learn to listen for and pay attention to God's voice;
- Feel excitement and awe as they realize that God speaks to them and has important things for them to do;
- Act by obeying God by doing one specific thing they feel He is telling them to do.

The Biggest Verse

"The Lord came and stood there, calling as at the other times, 'Samuel! Samuel!' Then Samuel said, 'Speak, for your servant is listening.'" 1 Samuel 3:10

Other Important Verses

Genesis 41:1-40; Exodus 3:1-15; 20:12; Numbers 22:21-34; 1 Samuel 3:1—4:1; 8:1-3; 2 Samuel 12:1-20; Psalm 19; 99:6; Matthew 5:27-30; 6:3,4; Luke 6:31; 10:27; John 10:2-5,11,14; Acts 9:1-6; Romans 1:18-20; Ephesians 4:29; Revelation 1:1,2

Samuel: The Boy Who Obeyed God's Voice

STEP
MOVING IN

This step reminds students that listening requires work.

Option 1  Move It

You'll need Paper, pens or pencils, small prizes (gum, candy, etc.) and one of your favorite children's stories, such as the Dr. Seuss classic *Horton Hears a Who*.

> **Option:** Replace the children's story with a can of Spam and read the ingredients and advertising on the label. Give a piece of candy for a correct response and give the can of Spam to the person who correctly answers the most questions on the pop quiz.

Introduce this step by explaining: **I'm going to read to you one of my favorite childhood stories.** After you read the story, then surprise the students by announcing a pop quiz. After the moaning subsides, distribute the paper and pens or pencils; then ask detailed questions about the story, such as: *What was the name of the first person Horton met?* Award prizes for correct answers. Discuss how students might have listened differently if they had known they were going to be tested on what they were hearing.

Discuss: **What would you have done differently if you had known beforehand that I was going to give candy prizes for correct answers?** Explain: **Often there are rewards for doing the hard work of listening, especially if we're trying to listen to the right voices. Today we're going to check out someone who was about your age when he learned that listening to the right voice might be hard work, but it really pays off.**

Option 2  Chat Room

You'll need Three portable tape or CD players and headphones, three popular music tapes or CDs, at least 30 3x5-inch index cards, a felt-tip pen and a candy prize.

Ahead of time, create three sets of score cards numbered 1 to 10 using the 3x5-inch index cards.

Welcome students to the new series about teens of the Bible; then discuss: **How much music do you think you listen to in an average week?** Determine which three students listen to the most music in an average week. (Don't be surprised if it's more time than they spend in school per week!) Then ask the three to come forward. Explain as you give each "volunteer" a tape or CD player that you are going to cue them one at a time to sing "Twinkle, Twinkle Little Star" while they listen to the tape or CD and that the best performance will win a prize. Instruct the contestants to turn the music on and adjust the volume as loud as they can comfortably listen.

> **Note:** Depending on the quality of the headphones, you should be able to hear the music while standing near the person wearing the headset—this will tell you if it's loud enough to begin the contest.

While the contestants are listening to their music, select three students to act as judges for the contest and give them each a set of score cards. Explain that they are to rate the performances based on volume, tune and entertainment value; then cue the first contestant to sing. After the last contestant performs, add up the scores and announce the winner.

Ask the contestants: **How did it feel to listen to one thing and do another thing?** Ask the group: **How did it feel to hear someone who was listening to one thing and trying to do another thing?**

Discuss:

What is one time recently when your parents told you to do something and you did something completely different from what you were told?

Why did you do something different from what they told you to do?

Additional discussion questions for delving deeper:

Can you think of a time when you felt you heard something from God and had to choose whether or not to follow what He was telling you?

What did you end up doing: what you thought God wanted you to do or something different?

Transition to the next step by acknowledging: **It's hard to listen to one thing and do something completely different. Today we're going to look at someone who was about your age when he learned firsthand the importance of listening to God and doing what he was told to do.**

Option 3
Fun and Games

You'll need One lollipop per student.

Ahead of time, write a different two- to three-sentence paragraph for every eight to ten students. For example: *The cowboys drove their herd through the dusty, red plains of Texas until they came to the bank of the river. There they made camp and enjoyed their first bath in weeks. Little did they know what surprises lay ahead for them on the trail.*

Greet students and let them know that you're starting an exciting new series on teen heroes of the Bible. Divide the group into teams of 8 to 10 students. **Note:** If the group is smaller than eight students, use the good ol' "students versus adults" stand-by. Large groups that make up more than three teams can have more than one team at a time play.

Explain: **Today we're going to play Team Telephone. When it's your team's turn, you will stand in a line; and I will whisper a paragraph to the first person in line, who will whisper the paragraph as accurately as possible to the next person and so on until the information is whispered to the last person. The last person in line will then share with the group the message that he or she heard. An important rule: No repeating the information—what you hear the first time is what you get!**

Here's the trick: The other team(s) will be trying to distract you as you are whispering the story down through your team. Other teams can do anything verbal—yelling, screaming, talking—to distract you from listening to what's being whispered in your ear. One last thing: While you are in line, each of you will get a lollipop that must stay in your mouth as you whisper the information to the next person.

Following the game, discuss what made listening to each other easy and what made it difficult. Transition to the next step by explaining: **Although listening to anyone, including God, often requires work, it is important that we learn to listen to Him so that we can know how He wants us to act. Today we're going to check out someone who was just about your age when he learned this in an unforgettable way.**

In a somewhat ironic twist, when Samuel grew older, his sons followed the path of Eli's sons and were involved in dishonest acts and bribery (see 1 Samuel 8:1-3). Because of Samuel's age and his sons' dishonesty, the elders of Israel asked him to appoint a king. Although God asked Samuel to tell the Israelites that asking for a human king was a rejection of Him as their ultimate King, He allowed Samuel to anoint Saul. This initiated a series of kings, some who were godly and some who weren't, and resulted in the division of Israel into two kingdoms.

STEP 2 — MOVING UP

This step helps students learn the importance of correctly listening to and obeying God.

Option 1  Move It

You'll need Your Bible, pillows, blankets and a chair.

Ask for a show of hands from students who didn't get enough sleep last night. (There should be plenty of hands, since you *are* dealing with teens!) Select one of those students to come forward to play the role of Samuel and choose two volunteers to play the roles of Eli and God. Have the student who is playing the part of God stand on the chair as he delivers his messages, and give the student playing the part of Samuel the pillows and blankets. Explain that while you are reading 1 Samuel 3:1—4:1, the actors are to act out their roles. Encourage the volunteers to ham it up when they act, and each time they have a line of dialogue they can either mouth the words as you read them or repeat after you when you've finished with their line (knowing junior highers' short memories and attention spans, the longer the line, the better it is to have them just mouth the words as you read them).

After you've read the passage, thank the actors for their performances and discuss the following:

Have you ever been awakened in the middle of the night? How did you feel?

How do you think Samuel felt when God woke him up? Confused; disoriented; groggy.

Who helped Samuel figure out what was happening? Eli the priest. This is a good example of the importance of asking others to help us understand what's happening when we think God might be speaking to us.

Why was Samuel reluctant to tell Eli what God was saying? Because God told him some pretty bad news about Eli—that he had failed as a father.

How did Eli respond? Although the news was painful, he acknowledged God's sovereignty and goodness.

What happened to Samuel as he became an adult? He became a prophet—a messenger of God.

What might have been different if he hadn't responded to God's voice and obeyed Him? He might never have developed the habit of listening to God and he wouldn't have been able to share God's messages; he might not have become one of the greatest prophets in all of Israel.

Option 2  Chat Room

You'll need Your Bible and two cellular phones.

Ahead of time, ask a parent or other adult to attend the session and arrange to cue him or her to step out of the room unnoticed and call you on the cellular phone a minute or two after you have finished Step One.

Begin by explaining how important it is to listen and pay attention when someone is speaking to us. The key here is to stall until the cellular phone rings. At that point, apologize to the group for the interruption and greet the caller: "Oh, hi, Aunt Debbie" (or perhaps use your senior pastor's name)! From this point on, the students will only hear or see your end of the conversation, so hone your acting skills to convince them it's a real call. Make it obvious that you are not really paying attention to what the caller is telling you by rolling your eyes, tapping your feet and periodically whispering statements like "I'm almost done" and "Yak, yak, yak" to the group. Keep saying things to the caller like "Yes, I got it" and "Right. I'm writing down the number," even though you're not writing anything down. After about 30 seconds, act surprised and say, "You want me to repeat the number to make sure I got it right? Well, to tell you the truth, I didn't really write it down." Act really embarrassed, apologize to the caller for your carelessness and hang up.

After the call, explain to the students how embarrassed you are and discuss the following questions:

Have you ever been in a similar situation?

How did you feel when it became obvious that you hadn't been listening?

What would I have needed to do to really listen? Shift my attention from the group to the call, and actually write down the information.

What might happen if you don't listen when someone is speaking to you? He or she might get angry at you; you might miss out on something really important.

Finally, expose the call for what it really was—a pretend conversation—and explain: **That was one example of how important it is to really listen to people. Today we're going to look at a teenager from the Bible who learned to listen a lot better than I just did on the phone.**

Ask for volunteers to read 1 Samuel 3:1—4:1 aloud; then discuss:

Why do you think God chose to speak to young Samuel rather than someone older? Since Samuel was young, he was probably willing to learn to listen to God's voice. Perhaps being young, Samuel didn't have as many distractions. He might have been more spiritually sensitive.

Why do you think Samuel didn't recognize God's voice? No one had taught him what God's voice was like. He didn't realize that God might want to speak personally to him.

Why was Samuel reluctant to tell Eli what God had told him? Because God told him some pretty bad news about Eli—that he had failed as a father.

How did Eli respond? Although the news was painful, he acknowledged God's sovereignty and goodness.

What happened once Samuel learned to listen to God? God gave him an important message to pass along and began speaking to him more often about other things. Eventually Samuel became known for his close relationship to God (see Psalm 99:6).

Option 3  Pulse Points

You'll need Several Bibles, a radio or stereo and candy or donuts.

The Big Idea
God speaks and expects us to hear and obey.

The Big Question
What does God expect from us as listeners?

1. God expects us to tune out other messages.

Read 1 Samuel 3:1-10. To help students really dive into the passage, you may want to ask different students to read the different parts: what the Lord says, what Samuel says and what Eli says. Explain: **At first, Samuel had a hard time listening to God. Today, sometimes it's hard to hear from God because of the other noises and voices in our lives. We're often too busy, or we're spending too much time listening to other people, but He wants us to listen to Him.**

To illustrate this, have someone turn on the radio and then turn the music up loud enough to distract students as you continue to talk about other "voices" that we listen to instead of God's, such as our friends wanting us to do something or our many activities or the newest computer game or the TV, music or radio. When people protest (verbally or otherwise) about the noisy distraction of the radio, turn it off and explain: **Just as you had to work hard to listen to me with the radio on, sometimes listening to God requires that we tune out, or turn off, other messages. If we don't learn to put in the effort to learn to listen to God, we will miss out on the things God has to say to us and the ways God wants to bless us.**

2. God expects us to obey His messages.

Read 1 Samuel 3:11—4:1. Explain: **When God speaks, He expects us to obey—even if it involves taking risks or making us uncomfortable. Just as Samuel had to risk rejection or possibly punishment in order to obey God's command to share His message, God expects us to act on what He tells us, whether in an audible voice, through His Word or through a Christian leader or friend. Then we will be able to better hear from God in the future because obedience leads to blessings and relationship with God. In contrast, disobedience brings negative consequences. The long-term effects of Samuel's listening to God was that his nation was blessed and he himself enjoyed a close relationship with God** (see Psalm 99:6).

Illustrate this point by asking students to stand up on their chairs and do their best imitation of a chicken. Unless you have an abnormally compliant group of junior highers, many will remain seated, giving you their best somewhat disdainful "What in the world are you talking about?" look. Give a donut or candy prize to any students who actually stand on their chairs and do anything that resembles a chicken. Explain: **So listening to and obeying *me* gets you food. Listening to and obeying *God* brings way more joy and fun and peace than we could ever imagine!**

STEP **3** MOVING ON

This step reminds us that God speaks to us today in a variety of real and personal ways.

Option 1 Chat Room

You'll need Several Bibles.

Ahead of time, write the following Scripture references on six 3x5-inch index cards, one on each card:

Joseph understanding God through dreams, Genesis 41:1-40;
Moses hearing from God in a burning bush, Exodus 3:1-15;
Balaam hearing from his donkey, Numbers 22:21-34;
David hearing from Nathan, 2 Samuel 12:1-20;
Saul hearing from God, Acts 9:1-6;
John receiving a vision from the Lord, Revelation 1:1,2.

Begin by explaining: **God spoke in a pretty incredible way to Samuel, but Samuel is not the only person to have such an amazing encounter with Him.** Divide students into six groups and distribute the index cards. Instruct students to brainstorm how each story might look if written today. Tell them that they will be performing a short drama to illustrate their ideas about how God might speak to someone today based on the specific example found in their assigned Scripture passage. For example, in the story of Samuel, they might interpret Samuel as getting confused and thinking he hears his radio that he had left on when he fell asleep. Allow a few minutes of planning; then have each group perform their drama.

After all the groups have performed, discuss: **Do you think God still speaks in these ways today? Why or why not?** God can still speak in the ways that He always has because He never loses His ability to communicate.

> **Note:** The suggested answers to the following two questions have been omitted to allow for the diversity of different denominations and doctrinal positions regarding ways God speaks to us today.

How does God usually speak to Christians these days?

In what ways have you experienced God speaking to you?

Option 2  Real Life

You'll need Nothin' but your good looks (and this great book)!

Share the following story:

> **You and your dad live where floods are common; but your dad, who is a very committed Christian, never lets the dangers of a flood worry him, because he knows that God will protect him. During one particularly heavy season of rain, your town is being evacuated because it looks like the whole town is going to be flooded. Your dad tells the policeman who comes to warn you, "Don't worry—God's looking out for us."**

> **Sure enough, the flood comes and forces you and your dad to the second story of your home. A National Guardsman comes by in a boat and yells for the two of you to get in and ride to safety, but your dad simply replies, "Don't worry—God's looking out for us." The flooding continues and the two of you are forced to climb onto the roof of the house. Just as you are both clinging to the chimney, a helicopter comes and lowers a rope. Your dad waves it off saying, "Don't worry—God's looking out for us." By now, you're getting wet, cold and scared.**

Discuss:

What would you tell your dad right about now? God *is* looking out for us! By sending the policeman, the National Guardsman and the helicopter pilot, He's speaking and working through them.

Why do you think the dad in the story didn't recognize God's messengers? He didn't expect God to speak to him through other people (even non-Christians). He had a limited understanding of how God speaks to us and provides for us.

In what ways did God speak to people in the Bible? All sorts of ways: a voice, angels, prayer, Scripture, dreams and circumstances. If you have time, have volunteers quickly flip to the passages listed at the beginning of Option 1, Chat Room.

In what ways does God speak to us today? Most often through prayer, Scripture, fellow Christians, circumstances and an inner urging, but God can (and does) use other means such as dreams, angels, visions and audible voices.

What should we do when we hear God's voice? Give God our full attention and obey whatever He commands.

What do we do if we're not sure whether it's God or not? Just as Samuel sought out the advice of Eli, we can seek out advice from other adults and friends who have a close relationship with God. Read John 10:2-5,11,14. Point out that when we have a growing relationship with Jesus, we will recognize when He speaks to us. Another test for whether or not God is really speaking to you is to ask if what you are "hearing" agrees with God's Word, the Bible.

Option 3 — Tough Questions

You'll need The ability to let your junior highers struggle with these challenging questions!

1. **Does God speak to everyone or just Christians?** God speaks to everyone, but Christians have the advantage of having God's Holy Spirit living inside them, as well as the Bible and the Church to help them hear and understand Him.

> **Note:** For examples of ways that God speaks to all people, see Psalm 19 and Romans 1:18-20; both state that God declares Himself through creation.

2. **In what ways does God speak to people today?** God speaks through creation, Scripture, prayer, other people, circumstances and the Church. (See names and Scripture references in Option 1, Chat Room.)

3. **How do we know when it's God's voice and not just our own thoughts?** John 10:2-5,11,14 testify to the fact that if we belong to Jesus, we will recognize His voice. This involves faith in God and a growing familiarity with Jesus, His teachings and His ways. Also, just as Samuel needed Eli's help, we need to ask for help from other wise friends and adults to learn how to discern whether it's actually God speaking. Another way to know that God is speaking to you is to ask yourself if what you are "hearing" agrees with God's Word, the Bible.

4. **Why doesn't God just let us know that it's Him by sending us an e-mail or announcing it on a loudspeaker?** Well, He *could* do that because He can do anything; but if He did, we might start taking Him for granted. Perhaps God wants us to make the effort and learn to seek Him, spending time in prayer alone and with others in order to figure out whether or not it's Him.

5. **What happens if we don't obey what God says?** We will miss out on the blessings He has for us and face the consequences of our disobedience. We will also be a little more "deaf" to hearing His voice and it will be more difficult to hear Him the next time He speaks to us. Fortunately, God is patient and forgiving and willing to give us more than one chance, just as He did Samuel.

6. **Why do some people hear from God more than others?** There are several reasons: They may have chosen to practice and work hard at listening to God like Samuel did. They may also have the spiritual gift of prophecy and therefore serve as God's mouthpiece (see Romans 12:6). The closer our relationship in Christ, the more likely we will recognize His "voice."

STEP 4 — MOVING OUT

This step challenges us to obey God as we hear Him speak this week.

Option 1 — Light the Fire

You'll need Several sets of dice, copies of "New Numbers" (p. 24) and pens or pencils.

> **Option:** If you are reluctant to use dice at church, have students individually pick a number between one and six before they look at the handout.

Distribute "New Numbers" and pens or pencils; then divide students into groups of four or five. Give each group one die and explain that each person in the group will roll the die and check off the corresponding Scripture passage on his or her handout. When everyone has rolled, allow a few minutes for students to complete the handouts; then ask them to share their responses. Close by praying that God will give students the strength and desire to obey Him by doing the things He has told them to do.

Option 2 — Fired Up

You'll need Copies of "Ears Wide Open" (p. 25) and pens or pencils.

Ahead of time, if you don't already have adult helpers, arrange for two or three adults (this would be a good opportunity to enlist the aid of a few parents) to help keep track of students while they are outside completing the handout.

Explain: **Now that we've seen how God spoke to Samuel through a voice he could actually hear, as well as all the other ways God spoke to people in the Bible, we're going to take a few minutes to let God speak to us.** Distribute "Ears Wide Open" and pens or pencils as you continue: **You're going to have 15 minutes to work through this handout and see what God might be saying to you.** Ask adult volunteers to lead students to a large open area such as a lawn or picnic area where they can spread out and work through the handout independently.

After a few minutes, call everyone together. Invite those who feel comfortable about what they wrote to share with the group. Let students know that it's okay not to share. Allow time for sharing; then close in prayer asking that God would give the students ears wide open to hear Him this week.

Option 3 — Spread the Fire

You'll need Transparent or masking tape, 3x5-inch index cards, pens or pencils and a door (a real one or made out of paper, cardboard or plywood attached to a wall).

Ahead of time, ask a student or adult volunteer to share a time when he or she knew that God was asking him or her to share about the gospel or personal testimony with someone else.

Explain: **One time when we can definitely hear from God is when He is opening a door for us to share our faith with others. He might tell us that now is the time to share or He might even give us the specific words to say.** Introduce the volunteer and invite her to share her story.

After the volunteer has given her testimony, explain: **The truth is that God often opens more doors to sharing with others than we may realize.** Distribute the index cards and pens or pencils as you continue: **Think of three friends or family members who don't know Jesus yet and write their names down on your cards; then pray for them, asking God to give you the courage to obey Him when He tells you to share with them.** Allow time for students to write the names and pray; then invite them to tape their index cards to the door as a commitment to be ready to walk through any door that they think God is opening.

Close by praying for every name attached to the door and ask God to speak clearly to the students when He opens the door for them to share His Word with their friends and family.

NOTES

New Numbers

Circle the number of the command from God that you have been assigned for the week.

1. "Honor your father and your mother" (Exodus 20:12).

2. Run away from lust and flee temptation (see Matthew 5:27-30).

3. "When you give to the needy, do not let your left hand know what your right hand is doing, so that your giving may be in secret" (Matthew 6:3,4).

4. "Do to others as you would have them do to you" (Luke 6:31).

5. "Love your neighbor as yourself" (Luke 10:27).

6. "Don't use bad language. Say only what is good and helpful to those you are talking to, and what will give them a blessing" (Ephesians 4:29, *TLB*).

Read the Scripture passage next to the number you circled and ask God how He wants you to obey Him this week, then write down what you believe He is asking you to do.

Write down what you need from God in order to obey what He is asking you to do and pray that He would use you to bless others and become more like Jesus.

Ears Wide Open

Ask God to speak to you through the following version of Psalm 40:1-8; then answer the questions on the next page.

I waited and waited and waited for God.
At last he looked; finally he listened.
He lifted me out of the ditch, pulled me from deep mud.
He stood me up on a solid rock to make sure
I wouldn't slip.
He taught me how to sing the latest God-song,
a praise-song to our God.
More and more people are seeing this: they enter the
mystery, abandoning themselves to God.
Blessed are you who give yourselves over to God,
turn your backs on the world's "sure thing,"
ignore what the world worships;
The world's a huge stockpile of God-wonders
and God-thoughts.
Nothing and no one comes close to you!
I start talking about you, telling what I know,
and quickly run out of words.
Neither numbers nor words account for you.
Doing something for you, bringing something to
you—that's not what you're after.
Being religious, acting pious—that's not
what you're asking for.
You've opened my ears so I can listen.
So I answered, "I'm coming. I read in your letter
what you wrote about me,
And I'm coming to the party you're throwing for me."
That's when God's Word entered my life,
became part of my very being.[1]

Do you feel a little like you're in a ditch right now? What might you need to do for God to lift you out?

What would it mean for you to fully give yourself over to God this week?

What is God looking to do in your life?

God is throwing you a party. What's it like? What keeps you from going?

How can you let God's Word enter your life and become a part of all you are this week?

Note
1. Taken from *THE MESSAGE* by Eugene H. Peterson (Colorado Springs, CO: NavPress Publishing Group, 1995), pp. 604-605.

Devotions in Motion

WEEK ONE: SAMUEL: THE BOY WHO OBEYED GOD'S VOICE

DAY 1

QUICK QUESTIONS

Flip to Habakkuk 2:1 and figure out where you should be stationing yourself!

God Says

If you were waiting for your best friend to call you any minute and tell you about a really cool party later that evening, where would you wait for the call?

☐ On the big couch in the TV room while watching a Star Wars movie with surround sound

☐ In the basement while you play a really noisy video game

☐ Under a big tree in the front yard, listening to your portable stereo

☐ In a chair by the phone

I Do

Sometimes waiting for God's instructions can be like waiting for a phone call. They can be really easy to miss if you're too busy listening to other things. Even if it seems boring or pointless, waiting quietly for God is really worthwhile if you're serious about knowing what He wants for you.

What kind of "noise" could be preventing you from hearing God's voice?

Ask Him today to help you to get rid of that noise and keep your antennae pointed toward Him.

FOLD HERE ---

DAY 4

FAST FACTS

Read Psalm 16:7,8 and get some instructions!

God Says

At night, Griffin has to do his homework, but it doesn't take much time. After that he plays video games or goes on the Internet or reads a comic book, but mostly he just watches TV and sits around, eating chips, drinking soda and talking to his friends on the phone. Sometimes when he goes to church he hears his pastor talk about a quiet time. Griffin thinks to himself, *It's such a hassle and I don't have time! What good is it anyway?*

I Do

A quiet time is important because it's easier to pay attention to God and remember Him when you're spending time together every day.

Do you have a quiet time? What do you do? Read your Bible? Pray?

If you don't have a quiet time, why not? Does it sound too boring or hard?

Would you be willing to commit to spending seven minutes with Him every day for the next week? **Caution:** If you do, it might just become a habit!

FAST FACTS

Try to find Psalm 37:7 with your eyes closed.

God Says

Gabby Gabberino loved to talk and talk and talk. She talked so much in class that she had to sit at a desk right beside her teacher Mr. Blank so he could keep an eye on her. She talked so much during lunch period that she never finished the lunch her mom packed for her. She came home from school, got on the phone and talked and talked and talked to her friends, forgetting dinner, her homework and even her favorite television shows.

I Do.

When you pray, are you all talk like Gabby or do you ever sit quietly and see if God has anything to say to you? Try it today, if you haven't before—you may be pleasantly surprised.

FOLD HERE -

QUICK QUESTIONS

Flip to Luke 5:15,16 and see what Jesus would do.

God Says

Imagine you have a big test to study for. What would be the best place and time to study?

- ☐ In the living room during the commercials between cartoons
- ☐ In your best friend's bedroom while she plays loud video games
- ☐ In the grocery store sprawled out in the middle of the ice cream aisle
- ☐ In your bedroom at your desk under a bright lamp with no music playing

I Do.

Like studying for a big test, having a relationship with God often requires both time and quiet. Time with God is very important but when you just "squeeze it in" you don't get all you could be getting out of it! Follow Jesus' model and make time to spend with God the Father.

Every night this week, think about the next day and see when you can set aside a small chunk of time to spend with Him. It will be worth it!

SESSIONTWOSESSIONTWOSESSIONTWOSESSIONTWO

The Big Idea

Getting rid of the idols in your life may require lots of changes.

Session Aims

In this session you will guide students to:

- Learn that there are many things that keep them from God;
- Feel hopeful about changes they can make that will help them grow closer to Christ;
- Act in obedience to the Holy Spirit to get rid of one idol in their lives this week.

The Biggest Verse

"The king ordered Hilkiah the high priest, the priests next in rank and the doorkeepers to remove from the temple of the LORD all the articles made for Baal and Asherah and all the starry hosts. He burned them outside Jerusalem in the fields of the Kidron Valley and took the ashes to Bethel." 2 Kings 23:4

Other Important Verses

Exodus 20:1-5; 2 Kings 22:1—23:30; Matthew 6:24; 1 Corinthians 10:13; Philippians 4:13; James 1:17

Josiah: The Kid Who Would Be King

STEP
MOVING IN

This step reminds students that there are idols in their lives that they need to get rid of.

Option 1 — Move It

You'll need Several large trash bags, masking tape and a bathroom scale.

Ahead of time, use the tape to mark a line on the floor approximately 10 yards from where you plan to instruct the teams to gather.

Greet students, divide them into teams of 8 to 10 and give each team a trash bag. Instruct each team to send the trash bag and two volunteers down to the tape line and explain that they will be collecting trash from their team. Clarify that you don't mean *real* trash but anything that their team is carrying or wearing that could go into the trash bag (jackets, shoes, socks, hair accessories, etc.) without unclothing anyone.

> **Note:** This game involves tossing items into the trash bag, so instruct students not to "throw away" anything breakable.

One at a time, have a member from each team come forward to throw an item toward their team's bag. The two team members holding the trash bag may move to position the bags so that items land in them, but they have to return to the tape line before the next team member can throw.

After everyone has tossed his or her "trash," weigh each bag and congratulate the team who threw away the most. Explain: **Usually the trash we throw out is more gross than this stuff—it's something we want to stay away from. Today we're going to look at a type of spiritual trash found in the Bible.**

Continue: **The word used in the Bible for what we might call spiritual trash is "idol." An idol is anything we put our trust (or time, money and energy) in apart** from God and His Word. In biblical days, little carved images of wood and stone representing pagan gods were worshiped with the hopes of securing a good crop, victory in war or healing from an illness. Today idols come in new forms but still draw our trust and focus away from God and fill our lives with garbage. Let's look at a story about a teenager in the Old Testament to help us understand why we need to trash the idols in our lives.

Option 2 — Chat Room

You'll need Just the real-life news story printed below.

Greet students and ask them to turn to the person next to them and share which household chore they hate the most and why. After a minute or two, take an informal poll of the most hated chores. Be sure to ask if anybody included taking out the trash. If nobody mentions this, you might need to check some pulses, then ask: **So, you all *like* taking out the trash?** When the group protests—and they will—discuss: **Why don't you like it? What would happen if you didn't ever take out the trash?** Introduce the following *true* story about one family who let its trash get completely out of hand.

Trashed Out—Couple relieved by discovery of their dirty little secret.

When authorities discovered the 33,000 pounds of garbage, trash and human waste in her home, Deborah Eggert said she was "relieved that the nightmare was over."

Mrs. Eggert, her husband, Michael, and their four children, ages 2 to 14, had retreated to tiny areas of their five-room home by the time their garbage-packed house and garage in a middle-class neighborhood were uncovered last month.

"I always thought, 'Well, I'll get to it, I'll get to it,'" she said.

A few years ago, Mrs. Eggert said, she began to feel hopeless about ever changing her life. She did less and less housekeeping.

"I guess you kind of get to a point where you give up," Mrs. Eggert said. "I'm having a hard time understanding how it did happen. But I remember feeling there wasn't anything I could do about it.

When I went into the house, I just blanked the mess out of my mind."

Now the Eggerts are trying to understand how they allowed their lives to run utterly out of control. In the months before the house was discovered, the entire family slept on a single set of bunk beds. Clean clothes were stored in the closet and stuffed into bureau drawers. A clear path led to the beds through putrid piles of soiled diapers, garbage and plastic bags of trash.

Without running water for the past two years, the Eggerts said, they washed their clothes at a commercial laundry. They carried home jugs of water from a gas station or nearby brewery. They stood in a plastic tub and poured water over themselves to wash. They went to the bathroom in plastic bags.[1]

Ask: **Can you imagine 33,000 pounds of garbage in your home? You might not believe that your own life could ever get as messy as that, but even this mess began with just a little trash at first. It can be the same for spiritual trash, too.** Ask for examples of some of the trash in students' lives that God would want them to take out. (You might need to give a few examples such as pornography, bad habits and selfish attitudes.) Continue: **The Bible tells us that keeping garbage of any kind in our lives can have serious consequences. The tricky part is that sometimes we want to keep what the Bible calls trash—idols.**

Explain: **An idol is anything we trust in place of God and His Word. In biblical days, little carved images of wood and stone representing pagan gods were worshiped in order to secure a good crop, victory in war or healing from an illness. Idols might come in new forms today, but they still draw our trust and focus away from God and fill our lives with garbage.**

Transition to the next section by praying that God would open students' eyes to the dangers of idols.

Option 3
Fun and Games

You'll need Lots of old newspapers, masking tape, a radio or stereo, some rowdy music and a bag of candy or gum for prizes.

Ahead of time, use masking tape on the floor of the room to divide it into four sections or quadrants.

Welcome students, divide them into four teams and ask each team to gather in one of the four quadrants.

Explain: **Today we're going to have an indoor snowball fight.** Distribute newspapers to the teams and instruct them to crumple it into snowball-size ammunition. Continue: **The object of the game is to throw snowballs into other teams' quadrants while you try to get rid of the ones that are thrown into yours. The team with the least amount of snowballs in their quadrant at the end of the game wins. When the music begins, you can start throwing the snowballs; when you hear the music stop, the game is over. Oh, I almost forgot** *one little thing*—**you can only use your feet to pick up and throw the snowballs. If you use your hands, you're out of the game.** Allow time for scrambling to remove shoes and socks; then turn on the music to signal the start of the game.

After a few minutes, turn off the music and assess which team has the fewest snowballs in its quadrant and award the candy prizes to the winners.

Explain: **It's fun to compete to see who can get rid of the most snowballs, but there are real life things that we need to get rid of, too. The Bible calls them "idols." An idol is something that is more important to us than our relationship with God—something so important that we might even worship it. Today we're going to look at a teenager in the Bible who was not only determined to toss out his own idols but other people's idols, too.**

Bible Bonus Note

As with many Biblical leaders, Josiah was a mixture of virtue and vice. After his great reform seemed to set things right, Josiah was reported to gain great confidence in God's restored favor. Possessed by great dreams of invincibility due to God's protection, Josiah went forth with a tiny army to stop Pharaoh Neco of Egypt, who was marching through the northern provinces. Not only was Josiah's military campaign thoroughly defeated, but he was also killed at

(Cont'd. on p. 33)

STEP 2 — MOVING UP

This step teaches that rejecting idols helps us know God.

Option 1 — Move It

You'll need One copy of "Josiah: The Quick Version"(p. 38), a white board and dry erase marker (or large poster board and felt-tip pens).

Divide the group into pairs; then explain: **If you're like me, when you were getting dressed today, you followed a few clothing guidelines, like deciding that you needed to wear two shoes, your belt should go through the loops on your pants and your socks should match.** Explain that today you're going to have a contest to see who is the best at breaking the clothing guidelines.

Instruct students to take a quick look at their partners and then stand back-to-back and change something about how they look that violates one of these rules (like taking off one sock or putting glasses on backwards). Tell them not to turn around until you give the signal.

Allow 15 seconds of back-to-back time and signal the pairs to face each other again and try to guess what each partner has changed about him- or herself. The first partner in each pair who states what has been changed is the winner; have him or her move over to the right side of the room and find another partner. Continue the contest, moving winners over to the right until you have two contestants left; then have the championship round.

After the winner has been decided, explain: **When we break simple clothing guidelines, there's usually not much of a consequence (other than looking slightly foolish). There are other rules that carry much more serious consequences when they're broken. A young teen named Josiah learned what can happen when you break God's rules.**

Read "Josiah: The Quick Version" aloud; then discuss the following questions and write students' responses on the white board:

How might Josiah have felt when he realized that his people had been breaking God's rules? He probably felt ashamed of his kingdom and remorseful for how far they had moved from God, but he also must have had hope, since he had committed himself to becoming single-hearted for God.

What did Josiah do to show his commitment to God? He got rid of all the idols and made sure the people began to obey God's rules.

How did this benefit Josiah and his kingdom? His kingdom was cleansed of the idols and evil practices and he saw the blessings of God for the duration of his life.

Summarize by explaining that in order to know God we must reject the idols we depend on and worship only Him (see Exodus 20:1-4). Even though he was young, Josiah modeled this important lesson.

Option 2

Chat Room

You'll need Several identical 50-piece jigsaw puzzles and one copy of "Josiah: The Quick Version"(p. 38).

Ahead of time, remove half of the puzzle boxes' covers and leave the other half of the puzzles with their covers so that students can still see the picture of the assembled puzzle.

Separate students by gender into teams of four to six. Distribute the puzzles without covers to the boys' groups and the puzzles with covers to the girls'. Explain that all the puzzles are the same and that the teams are going to race to see which team can put its puzzle together the quickest. The point of this exercise is that the students who don't have the picture of the finished puzzle to guide them will take more time than those who do.

When the first puzzle is completed (which should be by a team who had the cover picture), reinforce the point that it's easier and faster to do something when we have a guideline for what we are supposed to be doing.

Transition to the Bible narrative by explaining: **Today we're going to read a quick version of 2 Kings 22:1—23:30 that shows the importance of making sure that you always know what you are doing—more specifically, that you always know what *God* wants you to do.** Read "Josiah: The Quick Version"; then discuss:

Why did Josiah do what he did? He recognized that something was wrong with the faith-life of his kingdom; and when he discovered the Book of the Law, he realized how far he and his people had strayed from what God wanted them to be doing.

What was wrong with what the people were doing? Josiah realized that only God should be worshiped and that the idols were bringing destruction to his land.

These days we hear a lot about being tolerant and accepting other people's beliefs, including whatever god they worship. Was what Josiah did tolerant? No, but it was necessary to rid his kingdom of evil idols, just as surgery is sometimes required to remove cancer from a body. We are not supposed to be tolerant of the worship of idols.

Why would God be offended by the idols in the kingdom? Exodus 20:1-5 tells us that God wants us to worship Him only. God desires us to know, love and obey Him so that He can bless us and provide for us. Worship of anything else (idols) draws our attention away from God.

What happened when Josiah ordered a massive cleansing of the idols from his kingdom? He became known as one of the best kings ever to rule.

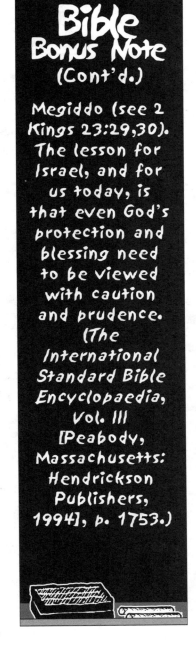

Bible Bonus Note (Cont'd.)

Megiddo (see 2 Kings 23:29,30). The lesson for Israel, and for us today, is that even God's protection and blessing need to be viewed with caution and prudence. (The International Standard Bible Encyclopaedia, Vol. III [Peabody, Massachusetts: Hendrickson Publishers, 1994], p. 1753.)

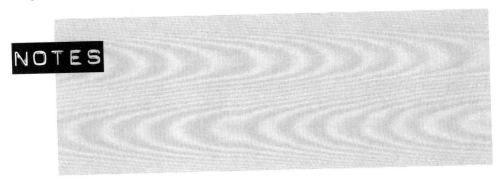

NOTES

Option 3  Pulse Points

You'll need Several Bibles, one copy of "Josiah: The Quick Version"(p. 38), aluminum foil, a cassette tape recorder, a blank cassette, an old blanket, safety glasses, a sledge-hammer and a visual idol such as an old TV, CD/tape player or VCR that you don't mind smashing!

> **Note:** The greater the actual value of the item, the greater the emotional impact, but you could probably pick up token idols for a few bucks at a thrift store or garage sale. You can even let the students take a swing or two if they are ready to make a similar pledge to rid their lives of idols.

Ahead of time, tape-record several young children's answers to the following question: "If you were made the president of the United States, what would you do?" Also ahead of time, wrap a Bible with aluminum foil and hide it somewhere in your room.

The Big Idea
God challenges us to get rid of the idols in our lives.

The Big Question
What idols do we need to smash?

Instruct students to open their Bibles to 2 Kings 22 and explain that you'll be telling the story of Josiah in a summary form, but they can still follow along in their Bibles. Read the summary of Josiah's reign from "Josiah: The Quick Version" and explain: **The story of Josiah demonstrates three things we need to do to smash the idols in our lives:**

1. Desire God.
Explain: **The first thing to note is that Josiah was thrust into a pressure situation because he was made king of a nation when he was only eight years old. His father had not left him with much of a heritage in terms of righteousness or politics, yet the Bible says that Josiah "did what was right in the eyes of the Lord" (v. 2). Somehow he knew that his future and the future hope of his kingdom depended on getting right with God.**

He wasn't sure exactly what that would look like, but he began by repairing the Temple of the Lord, and God honored Josiah's desire to know and follow Him.

Illustrate how rare this attitude is by playing the tape of what the children you interviewed would do if they were made the President of the United States. Not only will their answers be pretty cute; but also they will most likely *not* mention the importance of pleasing and serving God, as Josiah was determined to do.

2. Discover God's Word.
Introduce this point by explaining that you've hidden a special treasure somewhere in the room and invite students to try to find it. Once the Bible (wrapped in foil) is found, continue: **Josiah was determined to find out what God's Word had to say about how he and his people should be living. His reaction when he heard God's Word revealed how serious he was about knowing God and obeying His commands. He looked at his own sin and the sin of his people and immediately repented, asking God's guidance for change.**

3. Destroy idols.
Explain: **Josiah realized his life and his kingdom needed to be cleaned up before the kingdom of Judah could begin a fresh start with God. Throughout his kingdom, idols and evil religious practices had taken over the culture and thoughts of his people. Josiah knew that a dramatic break from idolatry had to happen, so he ordered a kingdomwide purge of idols and false priests. Idols were smashed, burned and destroyed and evil priests were killed or chased out of Judah. As a result of Josiah's dedicated actions, Judah experienced a period of God-blessed peace and prosperity.**

Illustrate the point by sharing a way in which God has helped you to break the power of an idol in your life. For example, you may have given up listening to certain kinds of music or watching certain movies or TV shows. Explain why you chose to keep your heart pure for God and how God has blessed you because of your decision (be sure to include some of the less tangible blessings: the peace that comes from knowing you did the right thing, feeling closer to God, the chance to share the change with others, etc.).

Bring home the story of Josiah by showing students the old TV (or whatever item you brought with you) and explaining how it could be an idol in one's life. Wrap it in the blanket, put on safety glasses and smash it with the sledgehammer.

Please take every precaution to do this safely. Keep the item covered with the blanket, wear safety glasses or goggles and have students stand a good distance away. When you are finished smashing the idols, dispose of the debris properly.

STEP 3
MOVING ON

This step helps students recognize the potential for idolatry in their own lives.

Option 1 Chat Room

You'll need A TV, a VCR, a video camera and blank video tape, a white board and a dry-erase marker (or poster board and felt-tip pen).

Ahead of time, call a parent of one of your students and ask permission to visit their house early and do a "video wake-up call" on the student. Make sure the parent knows not to tell the student about your visit ahead of time—and ask him or her to avoid the temptation of requesting any special cleaning up of the student's bedroom, too!

> **Note:** Ask the parent to be available to enter the student's room first to make sure you avoid any potentially awkward situations.

Start filming and get plenty of footage of the student's bedroom; then wake him and ask him to sing a special song or help him select a wacky outfit to wear while you all go out for breakfast (videotaped, of course!).

Explain that you are going to watch a special video starring someone that the students might recognize. Instruct students to pay special attention to every detail of the video.

After the video, ask students to call out everything they saw in the room while you take notes on the white board or poster board. Discuss: **Most of these things you saw in the video seem pretty harmless. How could they**

become idols or things that you might worship? Discuss the potential for idolatry for as many items as possible. Some examples: Makeup can foster extreme vanity; clothes labels can become so important that we buy clothes because they're "in"—whether or not we like the style; the phone can become our lifeline to friends; the computer can open a door to addiction to the Internet; etc.

Be sure to stress that you are *not* accusing the student in the video of idol worship! Explain that you are merely looking for things we all probably have at home that can become more important than God *if we let them.*

Conclude by asking: **Given what we've learned about Josiah, what should we do when we recognize that something has become an idol in our lives?** Get rid of it, at least for a while, until you feel you can handle it without it becoming too important in your life again.

Option 2 Real Life

You'll need Just this awesome, wonderful, informative book!

Read the following story aloud:

Alicia was a seventh grader who received a new computer from her grandparents for her thirteenth birthday. At first, she used it only a few hours a week to type out reports and papers for her history and English classes, but after about a month, she began to spend more time on the computer using the Internet.

Pretty soon, Alicia was on the computer two or three hours every day. Most of the time she was online in chat rooms with her friends. Her parents were a little concerned with how much time Alicia was spending on her computer, but they figured that not much harm would come from it. She obviously loved it; after all, she talked about her computer class constantly.

At the end of the semester Alicia's parents realized the real harm that could come from her computer. Alicia had always gotten As and Bs, but this semester, she had gotten all Bs and Cs. The exception was an A in—you guessed it—her computer class. Now Alicia's parents don't know what to do.

Discuss:
What advice would you give to Alicia's parents?

Should they take the computer away from her? Why or why not?

When can something good become something bad? When it begins to take over our lives and other good things begin to suffer.

What other good things can become idols in our lives? Clothes, food, makeup, sports, grades, music, talents—pretty much anything.

Given what we've learned about Josiah, what should we do when we recognize that something has become an idol? Get rid of it—at least for a while, until we feel like we can handle it without it becoming too important in our lives again.

Option 3 — Tough Questions

You'll need Your Bible and some dogged determination to let students struggle with these deep questions!

1. **If God loves us no matter what, why do we need to change?** God has proved how much He loves us by sending Jesus His Son to die for us so that we can be reconciled to God. God loves us in spite of our faults, but it's because He loves us that He wants us to get rid of the things in our lives that hurt us or keep us from being close to Him. God knows better than we do what will make us healthy, happy and fruitful. God wants to bless us, but we need to make room in our lives for His blessings.

2. **What is so bad about idols?** God has commanded us to worship Him only (see Exodus 20:1-4) and warns us that we cannot serve two masters (see Matthew 6:24); we must choose which we will serve. Idols cause us to value the wrong things or put too much value on neutral (or even good) things and steadily drift away from Him. For example, being physically fit is a good thing that God wants for us, but it's possible to attach too much of our self-esteem to our bodies and spend all our time working out or thinking about our appearance.

3. **How do we enjoy things without idolizing them?** We need to realize that God is the giver of the gifts we enjoy, and thank Him for them (see James 1:17). We also need to ask God and fellow Christians to let us know if we start drifting into idolatry.

4. **What should I do if I'm already struggling with idols?** God gives every Christian His Holy Spirit to overcome *all* temptation. Read 1 Corinthians 10:13. He has also given us a community of faith to encourage and support us.

5. **Is there anything that can never become an idol?** Anything can become an idol—even good things such as Bible knowledge. This is because idolatry isn't just a thing; it is an attitude of our hearts. Whatever is more important than knowing and obeying God is an idol—money, entertainment, popularity, grades, our physical appearance, our possessions, etc. Even Bible knowledge can become idolatry when we become obsessed with merely gaining knowledge and lose sight of the God who gave it to us, not allowing His Word to help us grow in our relationship with Him.

STEP 4 — MOVING OUT

This step challenges students to make specific changes in their lives this week in order to be closer to God.

Option 1 — Light the Fire

You'll need Nothing but this great book! OK, OK, we admit we're a little partial to this book!

If you chose the Chat Room option in Step Three, you can easily transition into this option. If not, transition by explaining: **Think about your own homes. What is something you have that has already (or might be on the verge of) becoming an idol? If you're not sure, think of one thing in your room (or home) that you wouldn't want to live without for a week. I'm not talking about things you need to survive, such as food or water, but something more such as your TV, stereo, phone or computer.** Share a personal example of something that has been an idol in your own life to help students become more introspective and vulnerable.

Ask students to get into groups of three and share about something in their own rooms that might have (or could) become idols to them—something that is more important to them than their relationship with God. Allow a few minutes for discussion; then bring the groups together and challenge students to make commitments to go without their chosen items for the next week. Acknowledge that it will be hard, but assure them that going without it for even one week will help them begin to free themselves from things that hinder their fellowship with Jesus, just as Josiah and his people became free by ridding their lives of idols. Close in prayer, asking the Holy Spirit to give all of you strength to get rid of the idols in your lives.[2]

Option 2
Fired Up

You'll need Paper, 3x5-inch index cards, pens or pencils and a clean trash can.

Distribute paper and pens or pencils; then ask students to write down an idol they can identify in their own lives. If they're not sure, you can help by asking them to think of something that they wouldn't want to live without for the next week (other than true needs for food, water and shelter). Explain that these things are not necessarily idols—yet—but they are a good place to start thinking about things that might be more important to them than their relationships with God. Be sure to clarify the difference between simply enjoying something and letting it become an idol. Remind students that an idol is *anything that is more important to them than knowing and obeying God*—money, entertainment, popularity, grades, physical appearance, possessions, etc. The list goes on and on. Show students the trash can and invite them to bring their idols up and trash them.

After everyone trashes their idols, distribute index cards and have students write down one way they can be sure to stay away from their trashed idol this week. For example, if their idol is TV, when they're tempted to watch it, they could go find a brother, sister or parent to talk to or they could spend the time in talking to God in prayer or reading His Word, the Bible!

Close in prayer thanking Jesus for setting us free from the bondage of idolatry and asking Him to help us recognize and turn from the idols in our lives. Encourage students to put their cards in a prominent place to remind them to avoid the idols they trashed.[2]

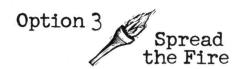

Option 3
Spread the Fire

You'll need A ball or other sport's item, a piggy bank, a school textbook, a yearbook and a makeup compact.

Ahead of time, distribute the listed items around the room on various tables, chairs or pedestals.

Explain: **One of the reasons that people don't come to know Jesus as Savior is because they have things in their lives that are already very important to them and they think these things will help them to meet the challenges in their lives.** Point out the items you placed around the room and continue: **All of these things can become idols: The sports item represents special abilities or talents; the piggy bank represents financial success; the textbook represents the idol of grades or knowledge; the yearbook represents the idol of popularity and friends; the makeup represents the idol of physical appearance.**

> **Option:** You might want to first challenge students to stand by the item that represents something *they* are tempted to put their trust in more than in Jesus. Give them the opportunity to silently confess this before praying for friends. Remind them that Christ will give us the strength to resist temptation when we ask Him.

Challenge students to think of a friend who doesn't know Jesus yet and stand by the item that most accurately represents the idol that keeps that friend from coming to know Jesus. Invite students to join with anyone else standing near their chosen item in praying for their friends by name, asking God to free their friends from the idols that are keeping them from worshiping Him.

If you have time, you may want to repeat this several times so that students have the chance to pray for several different friends who are trapped in idolatry.[2]

Notes
1. Adapted from the *San Jose Mercury News*, July 4, 1988, n.p.
2. For additional information on dealing with idolatry, see *Stomping Out the Darkness* (Ventura, CA: Gospel Light, 1993) and *Busting Free* (Ventura, CA: Gospel Light, 1994), both by Neil T. Anderson and Dave Park.

Josiah: The Quick Version

CONDENSED FROM 2 KINGS 22—23:30

It had been years since the glorious times of King David, and the kingdom of Israel had been divided into two parts: Israel and Judah. Currently they were both under the authority and rule of the Assyrians.

At the young age of eight, Josiah was crowned king of Judah after his father had been assassinated. Years later, as he became more interested in the faith and ways of his ancestors, Josiah sent one of his servants to provide supplies for the rebuilding of the Temple in Jerusalem. While the workers began their renovations, they discovered a copy of the Scriptures and brought them to their king. "When the king heard the words of the Book of the Law, he tore his robes" (2 Kings 22:11)—a symbol of his sorrow.

Josiah realized that he and the people of Judah had strayed far from God's laws by worshiping idols and following other gods, so he immediately sent his servants and priests to ask God what he should do. His servants found a prophetess through whom God sent the following message: "I am going to bring disaster on this place and its people, according to everything written in the book the king of Judah has read. Because they have forsaken me and burned incense to other gods and provoked me to anger by all the idols their hands have made, my anger will burn against this place and will not be quenched" (2 Kings 22:16,17).

Then God also said, "Because your heart was responsive and you humbled yourself before the LORD when you heard what I have spoken against this place and its people, that they would become accursed and laid waste, and because you tore your robes and wept in my presence, I have heard you, declares the LORD. Therefore I will gather you to your fathers, and you will be buried in peace. Your eyes will not see all the disaster I am going to bring on this place" (2 Kings 22:19,20).

Following these words from God, Josiah gathered all the people of his kingdom and read to them the Book of the Covenant that had been found. When he had finished reading, Josiah renewed the covenant to the Lord and vowed to obey with all his heart and soul all the things that had been commanded. Then the people of Judah pledged themselves to the covenant (see 2 Kings 23:1-3) and Josiah ordered a massive, king-domwide spiritual cleansing, removing idols from places of worship and breaking and burning them.

He also stopped the evil practices associated with idol worship by killing the priests of the false gods so that they would not lead people astray again. Finally, Josiah ordered the celebration of the Passover in Jerusalem, which was something that had been forgotten for generations.

Because of his commitment to God and his commitment to rid his kingdom of idols, Josiah is remembered in Scripture in this way: "Neither before nor after Josiah was there a king like him who turned to the LORD as he did—with all his heart and with all his soul and with all his strength, in accordance with all the Law of Moses" (2 Kings 23:25). Josiah reigned for 31 years before he was killed in battle with the Egyptians, and the consequences of Israel's past sins began to catch up with its people.

Devotions in Motion

WEEK TWO: JOSIAH: THE KID WHO WOULD BE KING

DAY 1

QUICK QUESTIONS

How fast can you find 1 Corinthians 8:4-6?

God Says

Which of the following would be the strangest to see? Pretty obvious, isn't it? How about the one that would seem the most *normal?* A little more difficult, huh? Well, it might be hard, but check off the one that wouldn't phase you a bit.

- ☐ A woman bowing to the ATM in the middle of the mall
- ☐ Your little sister kissing a poster of her favorite actor before she leaves for school
- ☐ Your best friend spending all of his money to buy CDs of his favorite band
- ☐ Your neighbor spending a whole Sunday washing, waxing and buffing his sports car

I Do

Even if you don't bow down or pray to something, it still can become an idol.

How much time, thought and money do you put into little things in your life? Is it even more than you put toward your relationship with Jesus?

Is there anything you need to stop worshiping today?

FOLD HERE -

DAY 4

FAST FACTS

Read Habakkuk 2:18-20 for a consultation of the wooden kind.

God Says

When it gets hot in Pinkerton, all the kids head out to the Pinkerton Towne Center to cool off, watch movies and drink frozen lemonades. The guys do tricks on their skateboards on the ramps and the girls giggle and look through the stores, never buying anything, just looking.

One day, Angie, a girl who loved the mall and spent all her time and money there, found out her folks were getting a divorce. As soon as she heard the news, she took all the money she could find in her room ($27.48) and marched over to the mall to spend, spend, spend.

I Do

What do you do when you have trouble?

- ☐ Do you get on the Internet?
- ☐ Do you go to the mall?
- ☐ Do you call your best friend or just cry in your room?
- ☐ Do you turn to God?

Sometimes we place importance on other stuff over God without even realizing it. That's called idolatry. Stop right now and ask God to help you get rid of any idols in your life that you turn to instead of turning to Him.

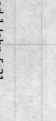

FAST FACTS

Be on your guard as you read 1 John 5:21.

God Says

When Will met Annie at church camp on the first night, he thought she was really funny and cute. But by Wednesday night, whoa! He was head over heels for her! He was skipping all the cabin meetings and worship times just to be with Annie and hold her hand. When the week was over, he came home; and the time he used to devote to his quiet times, he now spent calling Annie or writing her letters.

I Do.

A lot of people think of an idol as a big, dumb statue that people bow down and give things to. But really anything can be an idol, like a fancy car or even a person. An idol is *anything* that is more important to you than God.

Do you have any idols in your life? If so, are you willing to get rid of them *right now?*

FOLD HERE -

QUICK QUESTIONS

Hey, you! Joshua 24:19-24 is what you need to read! Hop to it!

God Says

When is it easiest to obey your parents?

- ☐ When you are really tired and just want to be left alone
- ☐ When you're worried about a big test coming up
- ☐ When you forgot to feed the dog and he is barking for some food
- ☐ When you realize how much you totally love them and want to show them that you do

I Do.

It is so much easier to obey and sacrifice for someone when you really, really feel a lot of love for them.

How do you feel about God? Are you bored or tired or are you totally in love with Him?

Pray that God will help you to love Him more and more as you grow with Him! The more you love Him, the more you will want to obey Him.

Teens of the Bible

SESSIONTHREESESSIONTHREESESSIONTHREE

The Big Idea

Even in a world that makes it challenging, following God's ways leads to His blessings.

Session Aims

In this session you will guide students to:

- Realize that God's ways are often different from the ways of the world around them;
- Be encouraged to follow God's ways, even in a world that makes that difficult;
- Take a godly risk in a tough situation this week.

The Biggest Verse

"But Daniel resolved not to defile himself with the royal food and wine, and he asked the chief official for permission not to defile himself this way. . . . In every matter of wisdom and understanding about which the king questioned them, he found them ten times better than all the magicians and enchanters in his whole kingdom."
Daniel 1:8,20

Other Important Verses

Daniel 1:1-21; Matthew 7:24-27; Romans 2:4; 8:28,38,39; Philippians 3:20; 4:7; James 1:2-4

Daniel: The Young Man Who Stood Up for God

41

STEP 1
MOVING IN

This step demonstrates the connection between following God and receiving His blessings.

Option 1 — Move It

You'll need One blindfold for every three students.

Ahead of time, create an obstacle course (or more than one if you anticipate more than 15 students) using chairs, tables, podiums, pillows and whatever else you can find (which in the average youth room might be some pretty scary stuff!).

Greet students and ask them to get into groups of three. As you distribute a blindfold to each group, inform students that they are going to go through an obstacle course. They may have done obstacle courses before, but this one is a little different; one person from each team will wear a blindfold while the other two serve as guides to help the blindfolded person get through the obstacle course. Here's the catch: Guides can only say one word at a time to steer the blindfolded member through the course. For instance, a simple statement like "Put your foot higher" would be broken up with the guides taking turns saying every other word. The guides cannot touch the blindfolded person; they can only command him or her verbally.

Send the teams through the course one at a time. Discuss:

How did it feel to walk around without the benefit of sight?

How did your partners' directions help you navigate the obstacle course?

How would you feel if you had to go through another obstacle course blindfolded but this time without anyone giving you directions?

Explain: **Trying to go through life without God's guidance is like going for a walk with a blindfold on and not having anyone to give you directions.**

Transition to the next step by praying and thanking God that He has not left us alone in the darkness but has given us Christ and the Holy Spirit to give us guidance

and specific direction from the Bible for how we are to live in the world. Ask Him for the ability to identify and follow His direction for our lives.

Option 2 — Chat Room

You'll need An adult volunteer, paper napkins and two batches of the same kind of homemade cookies—to one of the recipes, add an additional four tablespoons of salt to the dough before you bake them (make sure to keep the baked batches separate!).

Ahead of time, cue the adult volunteer to allow students to try a cookie while you're out of the room, even though you will casually suggest that they wait until you return.

Greet students, letting them know that you've brought a special snack. Place the plateful of cookies made with the extra salt in front of students; then act as if you just remembered that you forgot the napkins. Ask the adult volunteer, loud enough for students to hear: "**Oh, I forgot the napkins. I'll be right back. Just watch the cookies, OK?**" Then leave the room for a few minutes. Some students will be tempted and will likely try a cookie, in which case they'll be in for a salty surprise!

Return with the napkins and ask if anyone took a cookie. If any of them did, ask them to share how it tasted. If not, explain that the cookies have an unusual taste and ask for a volunteer or two to try them. You should have some interesting feedback on your culinary skills!

Bring out the normal cookies and let everyone enjoy them; then ask: **Have you ever been given directions for something and not listened or followed them? What happened when you didn't listen?** Make the point: **We don't always listen to what people tell us to do, and sometimes when we don't listen, we end up being sorry. Today we're going to look at a guy who learned that listening to and doing what God told him to do made his life a whole lot better, even though at times it was tough to obey.**

Transition to the next step by thanking God in prayer that He has promised to reward our efforts to obey and follow Him and asking that His Holy Spirit fill your remaining time with the understanding and courage to follow however God leads.

Option 3  Fun and Games

You'll need Copies of "Speed Sheet" (p. 50), pens or pencils and a tasty prize.

Explain to students that they are going to play a speed game. Distribute "Speed Sheet" (facedown) and pens or pencils and explain that when you say "Go," students are to turn the handouts over and follow the directions at the top. The first person to complete the handout will win a prize. **Ready, set, go!**

The trick is that the first person who *actually* follows the directions and reads the list completely before starting will see that the last item states: "Do not do the above items. You only needed to read them. You are done. Smile at the leader, so he or she will know that you are finished!" Be sure to look around the room to see who does this first, so you can award the prize at the end of the game. Acknowledge that student by nodding your head (or some other silent signal), but let the rest continue until several people reach the question that asks them to stand and spin. (If you wait much longer, the students who reach the end of the sheet first will moan and let others in on the gag and spoil the surprise.) Stop the game, announcing that you already have a winner. Introduce him or her, award the prize and ask the winner to explain the winning strategy.

After the hissing and booing subside, discuss:

What were the verbal directions? To read the directions before they started.

What were the written directions? To read the list completely before beginning.

Why was it difficult to follow the directions? Students were too focused on winning the prize; they thought they already knew what they were doing.

Transition to the next step by explaining: **Today we're going to check out a teenager in the Bible who learned that following the directions God gives is critical if we want to receive the blessings He has for us.** Pray, thanking God that He has given us Christ and the Holy Spirit to give us guidance and specific direction from the Bible for how we are to live in the world. Ask Him for the ability to identify and follow His direction for our lives.

STEP 2 — MOVING UP

This step helps students to see that following God's ways often makes them different from the world around them.

Option 1  Move It

You'll need Several Bibles, four paper bags, two different types of vegetables (such as tomatoes, carrots, celery or broccoli) a fast-food hamburger and a large order of french fries.

Ahead of time, put the vegetables and fast-food items into separate unmarked paper bags.

Divide the group into two teams: guys versus girls. Ask for four volunteers from each team to come forward to play Eat That Food! Hold up one of the paper bags and explain the rules: **One volunteer from each team will come forward and the girl—without looking into or touching the bag—will make an estimate on how many bites it will take her team to eat the mystery food that's in the bag. The guy will respond by bidding that his team can eat it using a lower number of bites or telling the girl that she and her team can "Eat that food!" The guy doing the bidding can get advice from his fellow teammates in the audience. If he tells her to "Eat that food!" then the girls' team has to eat it in the number of bites she bid. If he bids a lower number, the girl can respond with an even lower number or tell the guy and his team to "Eat that food!" The bidding continues until the guy or girl challenges the opposing team to "Eat that food!" or the bid bottoms out at one bite, at which point the bidding team automatically gets to try to eat the food in one bite (which is almost impossible). If the food is eaten in the number of bites bid, the bidding team gets 10,000 points; if not, the opposing team gets 10,000 points.** Complete four rounds of the game so that the items in all four bags are eaten. Congratulate the team that has accumulated the most points.

Discuss:

Which of the two types of food represented in the game is more attractive to you—vegetables or fast food?

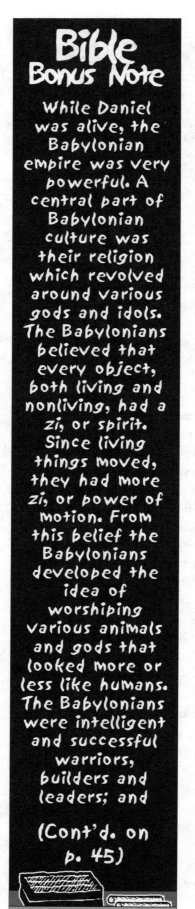

Bible Bonus Note

While Daniel was alive, the Babylonian empire was very powerful. A central part of Babylonian culture was their religion which revolved around various gods and idols. The Babylonians believed that every object, both living and nonliving, had a zi, or spirit. Since living things moved, they had more zi, or power of motion. From this belief the Babylonians developed the idea of worshiping various animals and gods that looked more or less like humans. The Babylonians were intelligent and successful warriors, builders and leaders; and

(Cont'd. on p. 45)

Which do you think would best nourish you for a long day at school?

If you had to eat either vegetables or fast food every day for three years, which would you choose?

Allow for some discussion, distribute the Bibles and ask students to follow along as you read Daniel 1:1-21. After verse 4, stop and explain: **The Babylonians conquered the Kingdom of Judah and robbed their treasury and the Temple. Along with the gold and precious items, the king of Babylon commanded that the best and the brightest young Jewish men be brought back to Babylon to be trained to serve in the king's court.**

Read Daniel 1:5-21, then continue: **Although it's not mentioned in the story, the reason that Daniel and his friends didn't want to eat the food is because they knew that it had already been dedicated to Babylonian idols. The Babylonians followed a tradition requiring that the first part of a meal should be offered to their idols and a portion of the wine should be poured out on a pagan altar. Eating the food would have been in direct contrast to the Jews' faith in God. By not eating the food, Daniel and his friends ran the risk of offending the Babylonian king, which could have resulted in their deaths.**

Ask: **How did God honor the young men's efforts to remain godly in Babylon?** He gave them favor with the palace master, kept them healthy and hearty with the simple foods, caused them to excel in wisdom and learning and placed them in the highest positions in Babylon.

Option 2  Chat Room

You'll need Several Bibles.

Ask students to imagine that Martians invaded earth and that all the teens have been captured and taken back to Mars. They have been given Martian names, Martian rooms, Martian clothes, Martian food and a Martian teacher (who fortunately speaks English) to teach them about Martian culture, so they can lead productive Martian lives as slaves to the Martian king, Zot. Ask: **What things do you think you'd miss most about earth? How do you think your faith in God would be affected by your being a Martian slave?**

Distribute Bibles and ask students to follow along as you read Daniel 1:1-21. Read aloud through verse 4; then explain: **The Babylonians conquered the kingdom of Judah and robbed their treasury and the Temple. Along with the gold and precious items, the king of Babylon commanded that the best and the brightest Jewish young men be brought back to Babylon to be trained to serve in the king's court. OK, so Babylon isn't Mars, but it was definitely a different and scary place for these young Jewish men.**

Continue: **Daniel was one of those young men. You may have heard the story of Daniel in the lions' den, but today we're going to see Daniel before he was in the lions' den—when he was much younger.** Read Daniel 1:5-8; then explain: **The reason Daniel didn't want to eat the king's royal food is because part of it had already been devoted to idols. To eat the food would be participating in idol worship. If you were Daniel and his friends, how do you think you would have felt every time you smelled the royal food and wine that everyone else was eating?** Probably pretty hungry and tempted to eat it.

Finish reading verses 9-21; then discuss:

Why did Daniel ask the guard to test the servants for ten days? He wanted to show that God was bigger and more powerful than even delicious royal food.

How did God honor the young men's efforts to remain godly in Babylon? He gave them favor with the palace master, kept them healthy and hearty through simple rations, caused them to excel in wisdom and learning and placed them in the highest positions in Babylon.

Transition to the next step by explaining that the story of Daniel demonstrates that God enables us to thrive *anywhere*. We might not really live on different planets, but we *do* live in a world that is vastly different from the original perfect and godly world that God created.

Option 3  Pulse Points

You'll need Several Bibles, a globe, a passport, a fast-food meal and a vegetable meal (a potato, carrots and broccoli or whatever else you can find in your refrigerator that isn't green *and* fuzzy!).

The Big Idea
God blesses our efforts to be godly in tough circumstances.

The Big Question
How does God want us to be different from the world around us?

While holding the globe in one hand and your Bible in the other, explain: **This globe represents the world that we live in. The Bible represents a godly and perfect world.** Hold the globe and Bible further apart and continue: **See how much space there is between the Bible and the globe? That's because after God created the world, sin entered and changed it. As followers of God we're still living in the world, but we're faced with all sorts of decisions about whether we're going to act like the world around us or like the Bible tells us to. Today we're going to look at someone like you who experienced firsthand the differences between the way people acted in the world he lived in and the way godly people should act.**

Read Daniel 1:1-4 aloud; then explain: **The Babylonians conquered the kingdom of Judah and pillaged their treasury and the Temple. Along with the gold and precious items, the king of Babylon commanded that the best and the brightest young Jewish men be brought back to Babylon to be trained to serve in the king's court. One of those young men was Daniel, and in the rest of this chapter he demonstrates two ways that following God's plan makes us different from the world around us.**

1. Our Devotion to God
Ask, while holding up the passport: **What is the purpose of a passport?** It documents your citizenship and is often required as identification when traveling in other countries. **What happens to your citizenship if you lose your passport while traveling in a foreign country?** Nothing—you're still a citizen of your own country, but you might have to prove your citizenship by some other means.

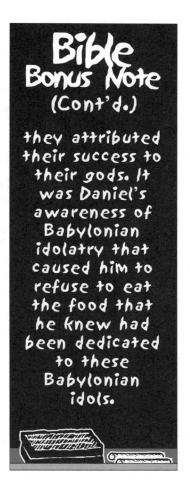

Read Daniel 1:5-8 aloud; then explain: **Although it's mentioned in the story, the reason that Daniel and his friends didn't want to eat the food is because they knew that it had already been dedicated to Babylonian idols. The Babylonians followed a tradition that required that the first part of the meal should be offered to idols, and a portion of the wine should be poured out on a pagan altar. By not eating the food, Daniel and his friends were running the risk of offending the Babylonian king, which might result in their deaths. Even though Daniel was in the foreign country of Babylon, he knew that his citizenship was ultimately with God's kingdom** (see Philippians 3:20). **He remained devoted to God even when it would have been easier to renounce that devotion and give in to the pressures of his new Babylonian culture. He also risked possible punishment. He didn't just carry a passport that said he was part of God's kingdom; it was as if it were imprinted all over his heart and mind!** Read the rest of the passage, verses 9-21.

2. Our Daily Choices

Explain: **Daniel was challenged to go along with what was going on around him, yet he chose to obey God. Even though everything in his life had been "Babylonianized," he remembered that he was one of God's chosen people and he could retain his godly citizenship no matter where he was by the way he lived.**

Hold up the fast-food meal and the vegetables and continue: **Just as you would probably choose this fast-food meal over these vegetables, Daniel must have been tempted to eat the rich Babylonian food offered him—especially since everyone else was eating it—but he knew that the food had been contaminated because part of it had been devoted to idols. Every time he showed himself to be different from the culture around him—which in this case was every meal—he ran the risk of injury and even death. God not only honored his efforts to live a godly life by keeping him healthy and alive, but He also caused Daniel to excel and become honored in a foreign land. He received all sorts of knowledge and understanding from God, as well as the ability to understand visions and dreams. Although we are not promised that the world will honor us as it did Daniel, we are promised God's blessings and presence as we obey Him.**

STEP 3 MOVING ON

This step gives students tangible examples of what it means to follow God in a world that makes following Him challenging.

Option 1 Chat Room

You'll need Copies of "What Can You Do?"(p. 51) and pens or pencils.

Divide students into small groups of five and distribute "What Can You Do?" and pens or pencils. Instruct students to figure out how many people in their group have consumed milk today. The group's total of students who've had milk today is the number that will correspond to their group's question in the top section of the handout. For instance, if three people have had milk today in one group, that group would read scenario number three in the top section. **Note:** If you have adult volunteers, ask them to join and facilitate discussions within the groups.

Allow approximately five minutes of discussion, then gather students back together as a large group and invite them to share their responses. Be sure to affirm each group for their ideas and encourage contributions from other groups.

Option 2 Real Life

You'll need Just the following story!

Monica was a seventh grader who had had a pretty tough year. She had just moved to a new neighborhood, started a new school and was trying to make new friends. It had taken several months, but finally she was getting close to a group of girls who had lockers near hers. The group was starting to talk about Sherri's slumber party and how much fun it was going to be. Monica thought it was going to be fun, too, but since Sherri was a new friend, she wasn't even sure if she was going to be invited.

About two weeks before the party, Monica found an envelope in her locker. It turned out that it was an invitation to Sherri's party. Monica was so excited. She finally felt like she had some friends.

The party was going really well until about 11 P.M. At that point, Sherri told the 10 girls who were there, "My mom rented us the new horror flick. Let's watch it!" The rest of the girls gathered about the television set, but not Monica. Monica froze, uncertain what she should do next. Although she really wanted to fit in, her parents had a rule that she could only see G and PG movies, and this one was rated R and sounded disgusting.

Stop and discuss:

If Monica wanted to fit in with everyone around her, what would she do? She'd join in and watch the movie.

If Monica's parents never found out, would that make it OK? Well, her parents are likely to find out somehow, and when they did, they'd feel that Monica had broken trust with them. Even if they never found out, it is wrong for Monica to deceive her parents.

Thinking back to the story of Daniel, what should Monica do and why? Just like Daniel refused to eat food he knew was wrong, Monica should probably let the other girls at the slumber party know that she'd rather not watch the movie.

Continue to read the remainder of the story:

Monica decided to speak up. She pulled Sherri aside and told her that she wasn't allowed to watch that kind of movie. Although Sherri was a little disappointed, when Monica suggested that they experiment with makeup and hairstyles on each other instead, Sherri got really excited about doing that. The girls spent two hours doing hair and makeup instead of watching the movie. As Monica was leaving the next morning, Sherri told her that she was glad Monica had the idea of experimenting with their hair and makeup and that she had more fun than she might have had watching the horror movie.

Transition to the next step by asking: **If Sherri or someone else at the party had made fun of Monica for not wanting to watch the movie, would it still have been the right decision?** Yes, we need to follow God whenever

He calls and wherever *He* leads, regardless of the outcome. Fortunately, God loves to bless us with the desires of our hearts and we often end up actually receiving the things we most fear losing (or something even better). But even if that's not the case, we have the peace and joy that comes from knowing we've done the right thing.

Option 3  Tough Questions

You'll need Just these questions!

1. **If God loves us, why does He keep us in a world where we have to make these tough decisions?** Because we live in a fallen world, everyone—Christians and non-Christians—will all be forced to face times of tough decisions. Fortunately, God promises to sustain those who trust Him and follow His ways. Those who disregard God's teaching, though, will be crushed by the times of crisis (see Matthew 7:24-27 for the parable of the wise and foolish builders).

2. **What's wrong with occasionally compromising our beliefs if God forgives us when we blow it anyway?** First of all, because it is sin—God will forgive us when we disobey His commands, but we are not spared the consequences. Cheating may result in getting caught and getting an F. Taking drugs may lead to an addiction. Having premarital sex may lead to pregnancy or sexually transmitted diseases. God is able to forgive us our sins; but our lives, and the lives of others, will reap the consequences. Every time we disobey God, we damage our own ability to hear His voice and see His leading in our lives.

3. **Why does it seem that worldly people often thrive while people who make godly decisions suffer?** While God promises that He will punish the disobedient and reward the obedient, this is not always obvious or immediate (see Psalm 73). God is slow to anger in order to give people the opportunity to repent (see Romans 2:4). Also, many times the consequences of sin are inner grief, loneliness, anxiety and guilt—all of which are hard to recognize from the outside, but cause inner turmoil. Similarly, faithful people

who suffer are often given "a peace which surpasses understanding" (Philippians 4:7), as well as the promise that God will bring good from whatever trial they face (see Romans 8:28 and James 1:2-4).

4. **Why am I not guaranteed a life free of problems and pain if I faithfully follow God?** Not until Jesus returns again will we live a life free from pain and trouble (see Revelation 21:4). However, God promises that He will be with us and never let us go if we give our lives to Him (see Romans 8:38,39). Those who don't follow God do not have the same promises; they will have to face the pain of life without knowing that God's love and presence are with them.

STEP 4

MOVING OUT

This step challenges students to take a godly risk in a current tough situation.

Option 1 — Light the Fire

You'll need Zippo, nada, nothin' but your good looks!

Ahead of time, assess how vulnerably your students tend to share with each other. If they seem comfortable sharing openly with each other, the following exercises can be done in pairs; if not, small groups of three to five students each might work best.

Ask students to form groups according to your assessment of their vulnerablity in sharing. Ask them to share with their group members about something that is on their minds, whether it is something that is bothersome or something exciting.

After each person shares, the other member(s) of the group will brainstorm a way that the "sharer" can act in a godly way. For example, if a student is really worried about surgery his aunt is having next Friday, the group might come up with ideas such as calling the aunt on Thursday night to let her know he's praying for her or volunteering to take care of her kids for free after school on Friday. Or if a student shares that she is excited about her drama audition on Saturday but a little nervous because her best friend is also auditioning, the group might suggest that she send her friend an encouraging note to let her know that she's glad their friendship is bigger than any part in a play.

Bring the whole group together and encourage a few students to share what was on their minds, along with any ideas from their groups. Close the time in prayer, asking God to give students strength to act in a godly way, even when others around them are acting different.

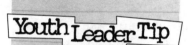

Youth Leader Tip

Often the larger the group—groups of up to five or six students—the safer and more anonymous students might feel, giving them the confidence to share vulnerably about themselves. More than five or six, though, has a reverse effect as students tend to become more like spectators than participants, causing them to clam up about the real stuff they're going through.

Option 2 Fired Up

You'll need Three 3x5-inch index cards for each student and pens or pencils.

Explain: **Every day, God gives us opportunities to make a choice to do something that He wants us to do rather than what the world around us expects us to do.** As you distribute three index cards and a pen or pencil to each student, continue: **On each of these cards, I'd like you to write down one way you could choose to do what God wants you to do this week instead of what others might expect you to do** (some examples: sitting with an unpopular student at lunch, not cheating when it seems like everyone else is doing it, or giving your favorite jacket to someone who doesn't have clothes as nice as yours).

Instruct students to turn to the person on their right. Each student will hold his or her cards with the blank side facing his or her partner. Each student will choose one of his or her partner's cards and give it back to him or her. Ask: **Are you willing to do what the card you wrote asks you to do this week?** Allow a few minutes of quiet prayer time, instructing students to ask God to give them the strength to do something that their friends might not expect them to do this week but that will glorify God.

After a few minutes, close in prayer, asking God to help students persevere in doing things that are different from what others around them are doing.

Option 3 Spread the Fire

You'll need 3x5-inch index cards and pens or pencils.

Explain: **There are lots of opportunities to share our faith as we make choices to follow God rather than the ways of the world. However, we often miss the chance because we don't share the reason why we are doing (or not doing) certain things that others are doing.** Distribute index cards and pens or pencils and instruct students to listen as you read the following real-life situations. As you read, each student is going to determine which situation to respond to and prepare a short response that would point others to God in that situation.

1. You were away for the weekend at a church retreat/event and someone at school asks you what you did this past weekend.
2. You're at a party and you are not drinking, smoking or doing drugs. Someone asks you to join a group that is doing these things.
3. You are part of a group of people who are beginning to talk negatively about someone else who is not there.

Allow time for students to prepare their responses; then ask them to turn to the person on their left and have the pairs share their responses. Explain: **We all have many opportunities to share our faith in Christ within the context of our everyday lives. What ways did you think of to show your faith in these situations?** Ask for volunteers to share their responses with the entire group. Ask: **What other everyday scenarios do you encounter where you have an opportunity to direct others toward God?**

Close in prayer, asking God to present each student with an opportunity to share his or her faith in Christ during the week ahead, and then give each student the courage to actually share why he or she is doing something different.

NOTES

Speed Sheet

Write your name on the line. Read the list completely before beginning.

Name: _____

1. Add the numbers 1 to 10 (e.g., 1+2+3+4...).

2. Turn this paper over and draw a picture of a horse.

3. Write three words that rhyme with clown.

4. Stand and recite the Pledge of Allegiance.

5. Count the number of windows in the room.

6. Write the names of three United States presidents.

7. Figure out the amount of minutes in two hours and two minutes.

8. Sing aloud the pig verse from Old McDonald Had a Farm.

9. Stand and spin in a circle five times.

10. Do not do the above items. You only needed to read them. You are done. Turn over your paper. Smile at the leader, so he or she will know that you are finished.

What Can You Do?

How many people in your group have consumed milk today? Find the corresponding number below and read the scenario aloud; then answer the questions that follow!

1. You are eating lunch with your friends and someone starts talking negatively about another friend who is not there.

2. You are part of a sports team where foul language is common and the coaches don't seem to mind.

3. One of your best friends has brought some alcohol to a party and has invited you and some others to sneak away and have a little fun.

4. Your friend invites you over to his house to play computer games and once you get there, he tells you that although he's planning to play some games, he also wants to check out some pornographic websites on the Internet.

5. You are dating someone who wants to push your physical relationship farther than you are comfortable. You are attracted to the person but don't think you should be doing what your date wants to do.

Think about what you have already learned about Daniel and how he was committed to living differently from others around him. Answer the following questions about your scenario:

How do you think Daniel would have acted in this situation?

What is hard or risky about acting this way?

How do you think others would respond to you if you acted this way in a similar situation?

What are some blessings that God might give you if you act as Daniel would in this situation? Remember to think not just about material blessings but also about blessings that relate to how we feel about ourselves and others around us.

Have you ever been in a similar situation? If so, what did you do? What do you think you would do differently next time something like this happens?

Devotions in Motion

WEEK THREE: DANIEL:
THE YOUNG MAN WHO STOOD UP FOR GOD

DAY 1

QUICK QUESTIONS

Our whole country could be changed. Don't believe it? Turn to 2 Chronicles 7:14 and see for yourself!

God Says

Now that you've read 2 Chronicles 7:14, which of the following do you think God wants us to do before He changes our country?

☐ Wear red, white and blue clothes for a whole week.

☐ Sing the "Star Spangled Banner" every day as we're walking to school (and when we say "sing," we mean belting it out at the top of your lungs).

☐ Admit to Him the things that we're doing that are wrong, and begin doing the right things.

☐ None of the above

I Do

OK, so you're not the whole country, but you are one person who lives here. And *you* can do what God tells you to do in 2 Chronicles 7:14. If you do, He will begin to change you and maybe even work *through* you to change others.

What do you need to repent of today?

How can you turn around and begin doing the right things?

FOLD HERE

DAY 4

FAST FACTS

Jesus said some pretty cool stuff. Flip to Matthew 5:11,12 to see something that relates to today.

God Says

You're having a great time at the sleepover at Robyn's house until someone suggests you turn to the cable movie channel on TV. The movie that comes on is rated R and within a few minutes you can see that it well deserves its rating. It has tons of swearing and violence, with some nudity thrown in for good measure. Your parents don't allow you to see R-rated movies, so you suggest that you all find something else to watch.

When your friends ask you, "Why? This movie's cool!" you tell them the truth—your parents don't let you watch R-rated movies.

They ask you once again, "Why?"

You respond, "They said it goes against what the Bible says." At this point, Robyn starts making fun of you, calling you a goody-goody.

I Do

Lots of times, following Jesus means people will say some bad stuff about you. They'll call you a goody-goody (or other names) and try to get others to join in, too. Jesus warns us about that in Matthew 5:11,12; but He promises that if we are persecuted, our reward will be great. We can't always be sure what that reward is, but we can be sure that God will come through on what He promises.

Today ask God to help you be bold for Him, even if it means others might think you are a goody-goody.

FAST FACTS

Quick, get to Proverbs 3:5,6.

God Says

Do you know what an "if-then" statement is? It's a statement that promises something that will happen *if* someone does something first. For instance, you might promise your cousin that *if* he lets you borrow his favorite CD on Monday, *then* you'll take over his chore of mowing his lawn next Saturday. Even though you meant the promise when you made it, on Friday a friend of yours invites you to go to the lake with him for the whole weekend and you totally forget about your promise to your cousin.

God makes a bunch of "if-then" promises to us, but unlike us, He keeps every single promise He makes. Like Proverbs 3:5,6: *If* we trust Him, *then* He will make our paths straight. Now that's a promise you can count on!

I Do.

What is one area of your life where you're struggling with trusting God? Maybe it's in a friendship, something that's happening in your family or something that's going on at school.

Right now, pray and ask God to help you trust Him with all of your life. *If* you trust Him, *then* He will make your paths straight.

FOLD HERE --

QUICK QUESTIONS

If you want to find out how to find something BIG, find Jeremiah 29:11-13.

God Says

When's the last time any of these things happened to you?

☐ You just realized that you can't find your house keys when suddenly they come flying across the room and land in your hand.

☐ You open your math book to turn in your homework and see that it's missing. At that moment, it comes whizzing toward you in the shape of a paper airplane and lands right where it's supposed to be.

☐ You're supposed to wear a shirt with your school colors for school spirit day, and just as you're opening your closet, it comes jumping off the hanger and lands on you.

Unless you live a pretty strange life, it's doubtful that any of these things has happened to you. When we want to find something, we usually have to go looking for it. The same is true with God. When we want to find God, we have to seek Him, just like Jeremiah said in Jeremiah 29:11-13.

I Do.

Stop right now and spend some extra time in prayer. You just might be surprised at what God shows you as you spend more time with Him.

54

The Big Idea

Following God means you care more about what He thinks than what others think.

Session Aims

In this session you will guide students to:

- Learn that pleasing God is more important than pleasing people;
- Feel an increased desire to please God, even if it costs them something;
- Choose one specific way to act that will please God this week.

The Biggest Verse

"'I am the Lord's servant,' Mary answered. 'May it be to me as you have said.' Then the angel left her." Luke 1:38

Other Important Verses

Matthew 12:46-50; Luke 1—2;
John 14:6; 15:18;
1 Corinthians 15:5,6; Ephesians 6:1-3;
Colossians 3:17; 1 Thessalonians 5:17

Mary: The Girl Who Risked It All

STEP MOVING IN

This step demonstrates that many times pleasing God conflicts with pleasing people.

Option 1  Move It

You'll need Three small bags of salty potato chips and one package of bubble gum.

Greet students and ask for three volunteers. Give each volunteer a piece of gum to chew. Allow a few moments of chewing; then announce that you forgot something. Hand each of them a bag of chips, explaining that when you say "Go!" they are to open the chips and eat the entire bag as quickly as possible—while still chewing the gum (this should be interesting since bubble gum and chips don't mix well)! Once they have consumed the entire bag of chips, each one is to blow a bubble. The first person to blow a bubble wins the rest of the pack of gum. **Go!**

Award the rest of the gum to the winner; then ask the participants to share whether or not this was a difficult task and what made it difficult. Transition to the theme of the session by explaining: **Sometimes it's difficult to do two things at once because the things we are trying to do are not compatible. The same thing is true when it comes to pleasing God. Sometimes pleasing Him means being criticized by others. Today we're going to check out a young woman who was about your age when she learned that choosing to please God sometimes means you won't please other people.**

Option 2  Chat Room

You'll need One copy of "Live Action" (p. 63).

Ahead of time, cut the handout apart into the 12 action descriptions.

Welcome students and ask for three volunteers. Explain that each volunteer is going to select one of the "Live Action" slips and act out whatever his or her paper describes. Then he or she will each choose *another* slip of paper and add that action to the first one. Continue until each volunteer is acting out four different actions at once; then stop them and ask:

Were you able to perform all of the actions at once? What made it challenging?

Discuss with the whole group:

What did you notice as you watched these three trying to do so many things?

Have you ever tried to do two things at once and found that you weren't able to do them both?

What did you try and why was it difficult?

Transition to the next step by explaining that it is *usually* difficult to do two things at once and that we sometimes experience the same kind of tension as we seek to please God and still want to please others. Rather than working to do both well, it is more important that we focus on pleasing God and not worry so much about what other people think. Explain: **Mary, the mother of Jesus, is a good example of someone who showed that she was more concerned with pleasing God than pleasing others even when she was your age—and she faced some major consequences for it.**

Option 3  Fun and Games

You'll need A long, sturdy rope (for Tug-of-War) with a piece of fabric attached in the middle.

To begin the game, pair off students with partners of roughly equal strength and send each partner to opposite sides of the room, forming two teams.

> **Note:** Be aware of any students who may not be paired off with someone of equal strength or size and subtly rearrange as needed.

Have each team line up for a Tug-of-War; then act like you are going to start the game. Stop suddenly and exclaim: **Wait, this is too easy! Everyone has played this game with their *hands.* Let's make it more interesting. You can only use your legs and feet—no hands at all. Anybody caught touching the rope with his or her hands will be eliminated from the game.**

You are now ready to begin. Give the **Ready? Set. Go!** signal and announce the winning team as soon as the rope has moved about five feet toward the stronger team.

Congratulate the winning team and let them all flex their muscles (leg muscles, that is) to show their pride. Introduce the next step by explaining: **Sometimes our desire to please God is in conflict with our desire to please others, and we feel a spiritual Tug-of-War in our hearts. Even though it might be hard, if we are *really determined* to follow God, we must care more about what He thinks than what others think. Today we're going to look at a girl who was about your age when she learned that lesson in a life-changing way.**

This step shows Mary as a model of someone who was more concerned with pleasing God than pleasing people.

You'll need Several Bibles.

Select four energetic volunteers to participate in a type of Charades. Invite three of them to come forward and one to exit the room to a soundproof location (you might want to ask another adult volunteer to escort her down the hall to be sure she is someplace where the group can't be heard). Ask students to suggest a silly activity that they'd like to see acted out by the three remaining volunteers. Help students to elaborate on their suggestions by asking specific questions. For example, if the suggestion is walking, ask for alternatives to walking (such as roller-blading). Ask *where* they might be roller-blading and suggest an unusual place (such as the grocery store).

After the silly activity has been decided, explain to the three volunteers that they are to act it out without using any words or sounds, just like the game of Charades. Bring the fourth volunteer back into the room and have the other three begin the action. Without anyone telling the fourth volunteer what the other three are acting out, instruct her to join in acting out what she thinks the others are doing. After a minute or so, ask the new person what it is that she is doing. The goal is for her to be able to identify the activity she is participating in; if she doesn't

know, have her continue the activity. Allow another 30 seconds; then ask again and, if needed, give her hints about what she's doing. If you have time, you can repeat this process with four new volunteers.

Thank all the participants and explain that this exercise demonstrates the power of *modeling*. Distribute Bibles as you explain: **As Christians, it's important for us to have people who model a growing relationship with God. The Bible is full of models we can imitate and right now we're going to look at a teen who modeled a sincere relationship with God.**

Instruct students to imagine how it would feel to be in Mary's position as you read Luke 1:26-38. Mary knew that God's plan for her to be pregnant before she was married would be socially difficult, but instead of pleading with God to change His plans, she submitted herself wholeheartedly to His will. It would have been tempting for her to try to persuade God to change His plans, complaining that she wanted to be spared the social consequences. Instead, Mary responded, "May it be to me as you have said" (v. 38). Mary modeled being more concerned with pleasing God than pleasing people.

You'll need Several teen magazines (such as *Seventeen, Surfing, Teen People,* etc.).

Ahead of time, locate several advertisements or headlines from the magazines that illustrate the pressure from the media to please or impress those around us. Look for such headlines as: *Five Ways to Get Her to Notice You, Hot Fashions for Under $20, Secrets He Wishes You Knew.* Also pay attention to the advertisements that suggest if you drink their beverage, wear their clothing or use their shampoo, people will notice you.

Begin this option by showing students the ads and headlines and asking:
Do any of you ever read these kinds of articles? What were you trying to find out?
Using the sample advertisements, discuss the following:
Have you ever bought any of these products?
Did any of them deliver what they promised by what they said or how they looked—the shiny, perfect hair or the boy or girl of your dreams?
What are these advertisements and articles trying to do? Ultimately, they're trying to make us want their

product; the way they do that is to show how our lives will be better and how everyone will like us more if we use their product.

Why do we want others to notice or be impressed with us? Because it makes us feel important, special and loved; our own insecurities cause us to feel better about ourselves only when others are pleased with us.

Instruct students to find a partner and share a time when they tried to impress or please someone else and why they tried to please that person. After a few minutes of sharing, read Luke 1:26-38 aloud and discuss:

Mary was a young teen when this took place. Do you think she would have read teen magazines if they were around in her day? Why or why not?

Do you think she ever felt pressure to "look good" in front of her peers?

How would she have felt hearing that God was making her pregnant though she wasn't married—*and still a virgin*?

Explain: **This is the kind of attention that you're *not* going to read about in a magazine. In spite of the social difficulty her pregnancy would cause, Mary was able to say, "I am the Lord's servant. . . . May it be to me as you have said" (v. 38).**

Option 3  Pulse Points

You'll need A set of earplugs, ear muffs, a kazoo, a radio and a large U.S. map. **Optional:** A crown or hat from a local fast-food hamburger restaurant and a burrito from a local fast-food Mexican restaurant.

The Big Idea

As followers of Christ, we are supposed to be more concerned with pleasing God than pleasing others.

The Big Question

What choices do we need to make to please God?

Read Luke 1:26-38 aloud; then explain that Mary, who was a teen at this time, made some difficult and important choices.

1. Choose to listen.

Explain: **The first good choice Mary made was to listen to God. She could have put earplugs in her ears** (demonstrate), **ear muffs to further muffle the sound** (do this too), **turned up her music** (turn music on at a moderately loud level) **and played along** (pull out the kazoo and hum along). **Mary could have done everything in her power to avoid listening to and obeying God when He spoke—but she didn't. The Bible says that even though Mary was "greatly troubled" (who wouldn't be?), she listened to the angel that was speaking on God's behalf and she was willing to allow God to work through her.**

2. Choose to say "No!" to the ways of the world.

Continue: **After she had heard the amazing announcement from the angel, Mary had another important choice to make. She could complain "Why me?" or boldly state that she was in no way going to participate in God's plan. The ways of the** world and her desire to look respectable probably would have made this option tempting—but Mary didn't choose it. Her relationship with God was more important to her, so instead of saying no to Him, she knew she had to say no to the ways of the world.

Illustrate the point with the map: **Let's say you were in Los Angeles and you're in a hurry to drive to Miami.** Show the general route it would take. **As you're driving through Texas, you come to a fork in the road and you have to decide whether or not to stay on the 10 Freeway or to head north on Interstate 99. You know you need to get to Miami, but the other route looks like a nice drive and someone said there's a great ice cream store just a few hundred miles up the road. Can you just decide to take the detour and still get to Miami in a hurry?** No. **Why not?** Because it doesn't go to Miami. **Can't you just decide to *make* that road lead to Miami?** No! **Of course not—you can't get to Miami in a hurry by taking a different road. You have to make a choice. It was the same way with Mary. She had to say no to the tempting road that would protect her reputation and remain on the road that led to God.**

3. Choose to say "Yes!" to God.

Ask: **Can you imagine going into a popular fast-food hamburger restaurant and ordering another chain's famous burrito?** Feel free to wear the crown and hold up the burrito. **That would be absurd, wouldn't it? By going into a restaurant, you are committing yourself to ordering from its menu. Silly as it seems, we do this kind of thing all the time in our walk with God. We try to listen to Him, but when He speaks to us, we decide we'd rather do our own thing. We can't have it both ways. When God speaks to us, we need to be ready to follow what He is telling us to do. Mary did—her eagerness to please God meant that she was blessed. Because of her personal choice and sacrifice, Jesus Christ was born and we were given a path to God. Amazing, isn't it, that over 2,000 years later** (and into eternity) **we continue to reap the benefits of Mary's choice?**

NOTES

STEP 3
MOVING ON

This step allows students to apply the principle of pleasing God in everyday situations.

Option 1
Chat Room

You'll need Copies of "What Would You Do? Really?" (p. 64) and pens or pencils.

Distribute "What Would You Do? Really?" and pens or pencils. Allow students five minutes to complete the handouts; then divide them into groups of four to six to share their responses. After five to ten minutes, discuss the handout questions with the whole group. Affirm thoughtfulness, creativity and honesty in the responses and ask: **What would be the cost for making this decision?**

Read Colossians 3:17; then ask: **What does it mean to do something in the name of the Lord Jesus?** It means that as His followers, we do it as if we are pleasing Him or acting according to what He would want us to do.

Explain: **This command from Paul sets the bar pretty high because it asks us to do everything with the attitude of pleasing and serving Christ Himself.**

Option 2
Real Life

You'll need Nothing.

Read the following story:

Emily was raised in a good home with her little brother. They didn't go to church, but the family had good morals and was part of several community organizations. Denise, Emily's friend from school, invited her to go to a church-sponsored pool party. Her parents didn't mind, so she went and had a great time. Soon she was attending many of the social gatherings and even decided to go to summer camp. While at camp, she learned more about Jesus and felt more and more interested in becoming a Christian.

Mary: The Girl Who Risked It All

When Emily returned home and shared her experiences with her parents, they had uncomfortable looks on their faces. Not knowing what they were thinking, Emily asked them, "What's the matter? You don't look like you want me to become a Christian." Her mother responded, "Emily, dear, we love you very much and don't want to get in the way of something you are excited about; however, we are concerned you are taking this 'Jesus stuff' a little too seriously. We don't want you to get your hopes all tied up in a religion that asks so much of you. You are on a great track in life with the promise of a great future if you keep focusing on the things that will get you ahead in life. That's what your father and I did, and don't you think we've done all right without God's help?"

Emily forced a smile and nodded her head while excusing herself to her room to unpack. Confused and a little hurt, Emily sat on her bed wondering what she should do. She didn't think her parents really understood who Jesus was and what being a Christian was all about, but at the same time, they did seem to have a point. Her parents seemed pretty happy and she certainly didn't want to disappoint them. Still, she just couldn't dismiss what she was learning and experiencing at the youth group as simply "Jesus stuff." Sitting on her bed, Emily thought to herself, *What should I do?*

Discuss:

What was Emily's dilemma? She was interested in becoming a Christian, but her parents didn't approve.

What were her parents concerned about? They thought she might undermine her success in the world by following God's ways. They thought that belief in Jesus wouldn't help her in the real world.

What risks would Emily be required to take in order to become a Christian? She would need to risk disappointing her parents and possibly being prevented from continuing in the youth group.

What risks would Emily take by ignoring God's invitation to become a Christian? She would run the risk of never becoming a Christian and spending eternity apart from God in hell. She would disqualify herself from receiving the Holy Spirit as her Counselor and Guide.

What should Emily do if her parents decide that she can't attend the youth group anymore? She should

submit to her parents' authority (see Ephesians 6:1-3); then take the matter to God in earnest prayer, asking Him to change her parents' hearts. She can even ask others to pray for her. Although her parents can prevent her from going to church or the youth group, they can't prevent Emily from having a close relationship with God (see Matthew 12:46-50).

Option 3  Tough Questions

You'll need Just these questions.

1. **Do I have to try to make God happy all the time?** It is not about trying to make God *happy*. God wants us to experience His way because it's the *best* way. He is pleased when He sees His children thriving, and that happens when we listen to and follow Him.

2. **Why can't we please God and people at the same time?** Sometimes people will be pleased as we follow God's ways—other times those opposed to God will want us to abandon His ways and follow *their* ways. This was true for Jesus (and the prophets before Him) and it will be true for us as well. In John 15:18 Jesus warns, "If the world hates you, keep in mind that it hated me first."

3. **Teenagers are supposed to have fun! Can't we just wait until we're older to worry about pleasing God?** No! That's the point of this study! All of these models from the Bible were teenagers *just like you!* God uses *all* of His children—regardless of age, which has little to do with the impact our lives can have for God's purposes. If we are old enough to wish we could avoid spiritual responsibility, then we are old enough to realize the importance of it.

NOTES

STEP 4

MOVING OUT

This step helps students choose one specific way to act that will please God this week.

Option 1 — Light the Fire

You'll need Several gift Bibles, a dartboard and darts. **Option:** Use paper rolled up into balls and a target drawn on a piece of paper.

Ahead of time, put up the dartboard (or target) where all the students will be able to see it. Begin praying about giving students a chance to make the decision to please God by asking Him to forgive them of their sins.

Explain: **Have you ever felt that no matter how hard you try, you just can't please God? You know what? It's true. You can try every minute of every hour of every day to please God on your own, but you won't because there's something that makes it impossible for you to please Him on your own: sin.** Demonstrate the attempt to please God with the dartboard and make sure you fail to hit the bull's-eye. Continue: **No matter how hard we try to please Him, we will never be able to do it by ourselves.**

There is only one remedy to our sin, one way we can hit the bull's-eye—Jesus Christ. God knows that our sin gets in the way of pleasing Him, so He sent His Son Jesus to light the way. Point out that as Jesus grew older, it was clear that something was different about Him. He could heal people and He even said that He was the only way to God the Father (see John 14:6). He lived a sinless life; unlike us, He *always* hit God's target of perfection. When He was just 33 years old, Jesus died on the cross, taking the punishment for all our sins. He rose from the grave, literally coming back to life from death, appeared before His disciples and 500 others (see 1 Corinthians 15:5,6) and returned to heaven to be with God. He became our bridge to the Father—our guide to hitting the bull's-eye.

Conclude: **Now you have the chance to ask Jesus to take over your life. To do that you must admit that you are a sinner, that you'll always miss the mark without**

Him and that you need His forgiveness to help you have a relationship with God again. Walk over and place the dart directly in the center of the bull's-eye to make the point and invite any students who'd like to ask Jesus to take over their lives and provide the way back to God, to surrender their hearts to Him and silently pray with you as you pray aloud: **Dear Jesus, I know I can't please God on my own because I'm a sinner. I need You to come into my life and take control. I ask You to be my Savior. Help me to follow You every day and please You in everything I do. Amen.**

Ask any students who prayed this prayer for the first time just now to talk with you after the session, and give them gift Bibles. Be sure to record their names and addresses, so you can follow up with them later in the week. Don't let the week go by without contacting them!

Option 2 — Fired Up

You'll need Several pieces of newsprint, several different-colored broad-tip felt pens, paper and pens or pencils.

Ahead of time, tape the newsprint on a wall where all the students will be able to see it.

Ask students to come up with a list of some of the things they have learned about what things are important for Christians to do (or not to do) and write their answers on the newsprint. Once you have a list, ask students to vote on the top five actions; then write them on another sheet of newsprint with a different-colored pen and spend some time discussing what these five actions look like. For example, "loving your neighbor" might look like sitting with the new student at school, sharing your favorite ice cream with a little brother or sister or raking the leaves in the yard of an elderly neighbor.

Once you have some practical ideas for each of the five actions, explain: **Sometimes it's difficult for us as Christians to act like Christians because we're too worried about what other people will think about us. In spite of the difficulty in overcoming our fears about what others think, our ultimate goal should be to please God.** Ask students to come forward and write their names next to any of the action ideas they would be willing to do, even if others might not be pleased. Close in prayer, asking God to help students care more about pleasing Him than pleasing anybody else.

Spread
the Fire

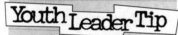
You'll need An adult volunteer and adhesive bandages (one for each student).

Explain: **The most important key to pleasing God is being in relationship with Him, and central to being in relationship with God is prayer. In 1 Thessalonians 5:17, Paul says to "Pray without ceasing"** *(NRSV).*

Challenge students that each time they hear a friend express a need (such as a big test, difficulties with parents or pressure from a big game) to volunteer to pray for that friend right then and there. Explain that their prayers don't need to be elaborate; they can simply ask God to be with the friend in a special way. Set an example for students by inviting the adult volunteer to share a real need with you and pray aloud in earnest for him or her.

Note: When you leave the pairing off up to the students, watch for those who are new or less likely to approach another student and subtly pair them up with group regulars who are outgoing and friendly.

Instruct students to find a partner and practice praying for each other. The first friend in need in each pair will be the person with the longest fingers. After sharing his need and allowing his partner to pray for him, the partners will reverse roles. When both partners have prayed, ask them to share with each other how it felt to be prayed for and how it felt to volunteer to pray.

Distribute an adhesive bandage to each student to keep in his or her pocket, notebook or book cover as a reminder that God wants to be near people who have needs. Encourage students to take the risk of offering to pray for their friends' needs this week and conclude by praying that they would be God's willing instruments of blessing to those around them.

NOTES

Live Action

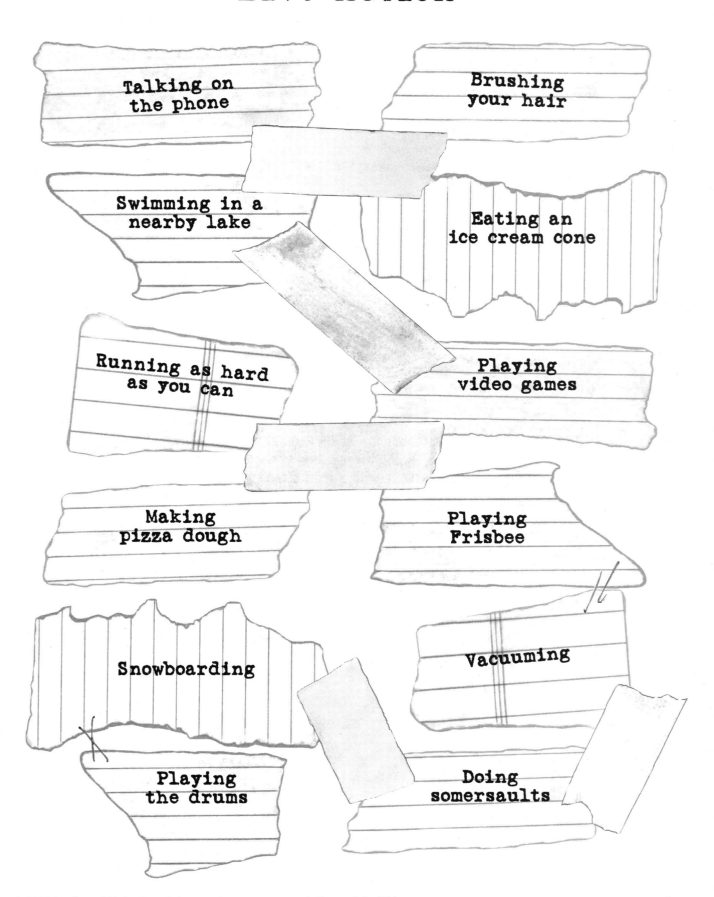

Talking on
the phone

Brushing
your hair

Swimming in a
nearby lake

Eating an
ice cream cone

Running as hard
as you can

Playing
video games

Making
pizza dough

Playing
Frisbee

Snowboarding

Vacuuming

Playing
the drums

Doing
somersaults

What Would You Do? Really?

The Gossip Gang

Your group of friends are hanging out after school when a couple of the unpopular students walk by. As soon as they pass, someone in your group says, "What losers! How could they be so weird?" This comment is followed by a story about one of the students, making her look even worse. You can tell these comments and the conversation will keep going unless something is done. What would you do? Really?

The Party Platoon

You're at a school party hanging out with some of your friends when a couple of popular students join your conversation. Soon they reveal that they've brought some beer and cigarettes from home and are planning a little "party within the party" out behind one of the buildings. Your friends act like they're planning on going, but they seem to be waiting to see what you are going to do. Everyone is looking at you to see your response. What would you do? Really?

The Cheating Cheerleader

You and your friends have spent the last few nights studying for a big science test. It's been hard work but you feel good going into the exam. Halfway through the test, a very popular cheerleader leans over and quietly asks you for the answer to question seven. You're not comfortable helping her to cheat; however, you're also concerned about ignoring the plea for help from such a popular person. What would you do? Really?

Devotions in Motion

DAY 1

QUICK QUESTIONS

Looking for a rest? Read Psalm 62:5,6 to learn where to find it.

God Says

Which would you rather do?

☐ Spend a hot Saturday afternoon on the beach **OR** ☐ Help paint a house

☐ Use your allowance to buy a new CD **OR** ☐ Buy lunch for a homeless person

☐ Watch television **OR** ☐ Call a friend who is having a hard week

☐ Hang out in your room and listen to music **OR** ☐ Hang out with your mom and dry dishes

I Do

When you care more about God than anyone else, you sometimes find yourself doing things that don't make sense to other people.

How concerned are you about what other people think of how much you love God?

What is one thing you could do to show that you love God, even if others might think it was a little weird?

FOLD HERE

DAY 4

FAST FACTS

Read Matthew 22:37. You'll love it.

God Says

It was the Friday before spring break, and everyone was talking about what they were going to do. "Man, I'm just going to hang around the house and watch TV," Jeff said with a grin. Andy told everyone he was going on a cruise to Mexico with his dad and stepmom.

Arthur stayed silent. He had signed up to build a Habitat for Humanity house with his older sister, Beth; and although he really felt like it was the thing God wanted him to do, he felt funny telling his friends about it.

I Do

Do you ever feel funny sharing with other people the things you do in serving God? Do you ever choose not to do what you know God wants you to do because other people will think you're not cool?

Ask God to give you the strength and courage to serve Him without fear or regret.

FAST FACTS

Hey! You're in trouble! Read John 16:33 to find out why.

God Says

Evan became a Christian when he was 12 at an overnighter with the neighborhood church's junior high group at the very beginning of summer. He had a great couple of months of singing worship songs, going to camps and hanging out with other kids from his church.

Then the first week of school came. Evan explained to all his friends from last year what had happened to him over the summer. He thought they would think it was cool. Instead they grumbled, called him "Church Boy" and didn't want to hang out with him anymore.

I Do

God never said being a Christian was going to be easy. A lot of people will treat you differently because of what you believe. What are you going to do when that happens? Are you going to stand firm with God? Ask God to help you share with someone today that you go to church or maybe even that you're a Christian. You never know what that might lead to.

FOLD HERE --

QUICK QUESTIONS

Turn to Psalm 77:13-15 and prepare to be impressed.

God Says

Imagine your youth leader wants you to invite one non-Christian to church this Sunday and these are your friends:

Caleb: If it isn't about sports, he doesn't care.

Linda: She would live at the mall if she could get a bedroom there.

Angie: She's kind of quiet and you don't know her very well yet.

David: He goes to another church on the other side of town.

I Do

Do you ever pick the easy way out when it comes to serving God? Do you ever care more about what your friends think of what you believe than what God thinks of how you live your life?

Make a commitment to *really* get out there for God by looking for a way that you can invite someone to church that you don't think will accept. You just might be surprised!

The Big Idea

Seeking out others to help you grow helps you to know God.

Session Aims

In this session you will guide students to:

- Learn that we all need help growing in our spiritual lives;
- Feel motivated to seek out help for their spiritual growth;
- Actively seek someone else to help them in the next few days.

The Biggest Verse

"'Why were you searching for me?' he asked. 'Didn't you know I had to be in my Father's house?'" Luke 2:49

Other Important Verses

Luke 2:41-52; Philippians 2:1-11; Hebrews 2:14-18; 4:15; 5:8; 1 Peter 2:2

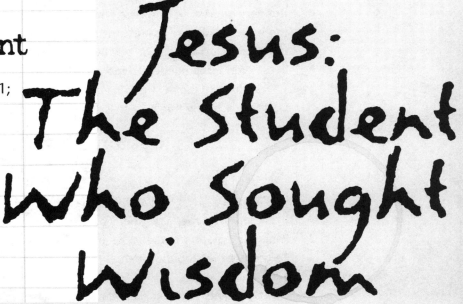

Jesus:
The Student
Who Sought
Wisdom

Reminder

It is illegal to rent a video at the video store and show it to your youth group without first having purchased a license to do so. A blanket movie license can be bought by your church that will allow you to show virtually any movie to your youth group or congregation for one year by calling the Motion Picture Licensing Corporation at 1-800-462-8855.

This step illustrates that we all need others to help us grow.

Option 1  Move It

You'll need Eye shadow, blush, lipstick and a chair.

Ahead of time, place a chair in the front of the room facing the students.

Welcome students and select three volunteers—one girl who knows how to apply makeup and two guys who (hopefully) *don't* know how to apply it!

Instruct the volunteers to come forward and have one of the guys sit in the chair facing the audience. Explain that the volunteers are going to demonstrate a makeover. The girl is going to coach the guy who is standing on how to apply makeup to the face of the guy who's sitting down. The all-important rule: The girl can *only* give verbal instructions—no showing how it's done.

When the makeover is complete, ask the rest of the group to rate the makeover on a scale of 1 to 10 (remember to clarify that people are voting on the quality of the makeup job, not the obvious beauty of the person who had the makeover).

Ask the volunteer who applied the makeup: **How did it feel doing something new in front of everyone? How did you feel about the help you received? Would you rather have done it on your own?**

Explain: **Sometimes doing something new can feel embarrassing since we're not very good at it; however, that's how we learn. Learning new things and growing in new skills are essential for a life. This is true not only in the physical, emotional and social parts of our lives; but it is also true in the spiritual part of our lives. Even Jesus needed to learn and grow in maturity when He was a teenager.**

Transition to the next step by praying for the lesson and your time together, asking God to teach new things so that students can grow and mature in their faith.

Option 2  Chat Room

You'll need A TV, a VCR and the video *Footloose*.

Ahead of time, cue the video approximately 59 minutes from the opening Paramount graphic to the scene in which Kevin Bacon teaches his friend how to dance. Be prepared to stop the video at the end of this scene.

Greet students and explain: **It's fun to see movie stars when they were a lot younger. I'm going to show you a clip of Kevin Bacon in a popular movie from the early 1980s called** *Footloose*.

After the clip is over, discuss:

What did the friend want to learn to do? He wanted to be able to dance without looking like a fool.

What kept him from learning to dance on his own? He didn't have the natural abilities to pick it up on his own and he was too embarrassed to ask for help.

How did his friend help? He taught him to dance using three important strategies: (1) he created a safe environment for his friend to learn; (2) he modeled the actions for him; (3) he tailored his teaching to his friend's needs.

What was the end result of their dance lessons? Not only did the friend learn to dance, but their friendship was also deepened and they felt good about themselves for what they had accomplished together.

Explain: **Becoming experienced in something new—including the process of growing spiritually—can be a little overwhelming when you're just beginning. Learning anything new is easier and more effective with the help of others who have more experience. When we study Jesus as a teenager, we see that although He was the Messiah sent from heaven, even *He* looked to others as He grew spiritually.**

Option 3  Fun and Games

You'll need Three of each of the following items: a three-course meal of pureed baby food in jars (such as chicken, peas and peaches), a bib (or a big towel), a baby spoon, a baby bottle filled with milk and a paper or plastic grocery bag. Also have three chairs, a plastic tarp and two prizes for the winning team (such as two big lollipops or stuffed animals—something you might give a little kid).

Ahead of time, place one identical set of items in each of the three bags. Set up three chairs on top of the plastic tarp facing the audience.

After you welcome students, ask for six volunteers to play a food game. (Don't let them see that the food you are talking about is baby food.) Pair up the volunteers and designate one person on each team as the "baby" who will sit in the chair and the other as the "parent."

The contest is simple: Each team's goal is for the baby to eat all the food and drink the bottle of milk as quickly as possible. There are only two rules: (1) babies cannot feed themselves—each parent must feed his or her baby the entire contents of all three food jars as well as the bottle of milk; (2) spilled food must be scooped up and eaten or licked up by the baby. Put the bibs on the babies and start the game. Award the prize to the first team to finish the meal.

Transition to the next step by explaining: **None of us would survive if we hadn't had lots of help from others during our infant years. Even the simplest tasks like eating are impossible for an infant without help. This is true for us when we are spiritual newborns, too; we need help from spiritually mature Christians in learning the basics of Christian living. As we'll see today, even Jesus Himself sought out others as He was growing spiritually.**

Youth Leader Tip

All too often there's a long-standing rivalry between youth workers and church custodians. We tend to make the messes, and they have to mop them up the next day. Much of this would be alleviated if you kept a large plastic tarp handy for games like this that have the potential of leaving gooey messes on the floor. Thirty seconds of work on your part today can save thirty minutes of work for someone (maybe even you!) tomorrow.

NOTES

Jesus: The Student Who Sought Wisdom

STEP 2 — MOVING UP

This step shows that everyone needs to seek out environments that help them grow.

Option 1  Move It

You'll need Several rolls of toilet paper of different colors and patterns and several different-colored felt-tip pens.

Divide students into groups of six or seven; then explain: **Although most of what we know of Jesus was when He was between ages 30 and 33, I want you to imagine what Jesus would have been like as a teenager. Think silently about that for a few seconds. Do you think He would have liked sports? Enjoyed candy? Thought girls were cute?**

Continue as you distribute a roll of toilet paper and pens or pencils to each group: **I'm going to give each group several different colors of pens and some toilet paper. In each group, the person who has eaten most recently will be "Teenage Jesus." The rest of you can use the toilet paper to give your "Teenage Jesus" the clothes you think He would have worn in His day and anything else that would relate to Him at your age.** Allow five or so minutes for students to work; then ask each group to present its own version of "Teenage Jesus."

Be sure to make the point that Jesus was a real-life teenager who, although He was perfect and didn't sin, was still a lot like us. He probably had friends who were His own age, He probably did chores at home, and He might even have had body odor every once in a while. Explain: **So far, our versions of Jesus as a teenager have come from our own imaginations, but we can learn a little more about Him at that age from the Bible.** Read Luke 2:41-52 and explain: **In this passage we see Jesus as a 12-year-old. He was on the edge of becoming an adult in Jewish culture** (which is age 13). **He had probably been to Jerusalem every year of His life for the Passover Feast; but during this trip, Jesus made it a point to spend time with the teachers and leaders of the Temple in Jerusalem, grappling with the tough questions of the Torah.** Point out that, in those days, Jerusalem was the center of Jewish culture and religious life. Continue: **Jewish teachers taught their classes in the Temple courts by asking questions, but it was also important for students to ask insightful questions. The unusual thing was that Jesus was asking amazingly insightful questions at such a young age.**

NOTES

Option 2  Chat Room

You'll need A white board, a dry-erase marker and this wonderful, awesome resource we call **Pulse!**

Explain: **Usually the paintings that we see of Jesus show Him as a little baby, a child or an adult. There's one stage of His life that not much has been written about: Jesus as a teenager. Believe it or not, to get to adulthood, Jesus had to go through His teenage years just like you do.**

Ask students to name some common things they do almost every day and write their responses on the white board. Typical answers might include: eat breakfast, brush their teeth, bathe or shower, clean up their rooms, empty the trash, feed the animals, go to school, etc.

After creating a list of things teens might do in a typical day, ask: **How many of these things do you think Jesus had to do, too?** Make sure you affirm any answers that point to His humanity: He had to do chores, He had to study, etc. Point out that Jesus was a "normal" teenager—He probably hung out with friends and enjoyed eating sweets and working in His dad's carpentry shop. Explain: **The only difference between Jesus as a teenager and you is that Jesus never sinned.**

So far we've discussed what Jesus was *probably* like. There is one thing we know for sure about Jesus as a teenager. Read the story of Jesus at the Temple from Luke 2:41-52 and explain: **In Jewish culture, a young man became an adult at 13 and Jesus wanted to be spiritually ready for the challenges ahead of Him. So while He was in the center of Jewish culture and religious life in Jerusalem for the Passover Feast, He made it a point to spend time with the teachers and leaders of the Temple, grappling with the tough questions of the Torah.**

Discuss:

How would you have felt if you were Mary or Joseph and couldn't find your son? Angry, guilty, scared.

What did people at the Temple think of Jesus? They were "amazed" at His understanding.

Why do you think His parents were "astonished" when they saw Jesus? They were probably surprised to see Jesus there, sitting at the Temple and talking intelligently with people who were much older than He was.

Why would Jesus call the Temple His Father's house? Isn't Joseph His father? Joseph was the father that He lived with; God was Jesus' heavenly Father. Plus Jesus *is* the actual Son of God, giving Him even more reason to call the Temple His Dad's home. Jesus had a unique relationship with the Father, yet He taught His followers to pray "Abba, Father."

So was Jesus disobeying His parents? No, because in verse 51, we see that He did want to obey His parents. His first loyalty, though, was to His heavenly Father.

How do you think other teenagers would have described Jesus? Smart, a goody-goody.

Explain: **Jesus took the initiative in seeking out the help He needed in order to grow closer to God the Father. Even Jesus depended on others to help Him know, love and follow God.**

Option 3  Pulse Points

You'll need Your Bible, a broken watch and a superhero action figure.

The Big Idea

We need other believers to help us grow spiritually.

The Big Question

Why can't I grow spiritually all on my own?

C.O.W. provides the structure here (feel free to have fun with that acronym!).

1. C—Created: God created us to need others.

Read Luke 2:41-52 aloud and explain: **In this passage we see Jesus as a 12-year-old. He was on the edge of becoming an adult in Jewish culture** (which is age 13). **He had probably been to Jerusalem every year of His life for the Passover Feast; but during this trip, Jesus made it a point to spend time with the teachers and leaders of the Temple in Jerusalem, grappling with the tough questions of the Torah.** Point out that in those days, Jerusalem was the center of Jewish culture and religious life. Continue: **Jewish teachers taught their classes in the Temple courts by asking questions, but it was also important for students to ask insightful questions. The unusual thing was that Jesus was asking amazingly insightful questions at such a young age.**

Illustrate this by sharing one area in your own life in which you have needed others to help you grow.

2. O—Ongoing: Our need for help is ongoing.

Hold up the broken watch and ask students if they can tell you something about it. Invite them to look closer and they'll recognize that it's broken. Explain: **Actually, the watch isn't completely broken because it's correct two times a day! However, for the watch to be correct throughout the entire day, its movement needs to be ongoing. Just like the watch, our need both for growth and help is ongoing. We will never get to a point where we won't need help from other people in our spiritual life. It may look differently at different stages in our lives, but if we don't keep growing, we'll be like the watch—not as helpful as we could be.**

3. W—Whomever: We can get help from whomever God provides.

Conclude: **We need to be open to getting help from the people God puts in our lives. Often we think that if we are going to get help, we need to find a spiritual superhero** (hold up the action figure). **We think our spiritual helper needs to pray faster than speeding gossip, have more spiritual power than a trainload of pastors and be able to take leaps of faith over towering challenges. God, however, often uses the normal, everyday "regular" people in our church to provide just the right help when we need it. If you know a spiritual superhero, go ahead and ask for his or her help; but don't deny yourself the opportunity of being helped by one of the regular mature Christians. You'll be amazed at how God can do miracles through all types of other Christians!**

NOTES

STEP 3
MOVING ON

This step demonstrates that we grow when we seek help from others.

Option 1
Chat Room

You'll need Copies of "Cool Coach" (p. 76), thank-you notes and pens or pencils.

To start this off, tell students about a time that you were on a sports team. Describe one of your coaches and how that person helped you in your sport. If you were never on a sports team, describe a recent sporting event you watched and how important the coach was and explain: **Just like athletes learn from their coaches, we often have people in our lives who are like coaches for our spiritual lives.** Ask students to think for a moment about someone in their lives who has helped them to grow spiritually. Distribute "Cool Coach" and pens or pencils and ask students to take a few minutes to write as much detail about their friendships with their coaches as possible. **Note:** Some students may not have had a "cool coach" in their spiritual lives. If this is the case, suggest they use someone who has helped them learn something in any field (sports, music, school, etc). Skills taught by parents will work, too.

Allow students a few minutes to complete their handouts; then discuss:

How did some of you get to know your coaches?

What were some of the areas in which you were helped?

What were some of the ways in which you received help?

Explain: **Almost all of us can point to someone who has been a help to us. Most of us were fortunate to have the friendship without too much work on our part. However, as we get older, God wants us to take more responsibility in seeking out spiritual help.**

Distribute the thank-you notes and continue: **Along with receiving spiritual help, it is important for us to thank the people God has used to bless us. You can do that right now on this note and send it to that special** coach or you can keep it as a reminder to thank God for him or her.

Option 2 Real Life

You'll need A TV, a VCR, and the video *The Empire Strikes Back*.

Ahead of time, cue the video to approximately 1 hour and 7 minutes from the second 20th Century Graphic (on the Special Edition version), to the scene in which Luke Skywalker is being trained by Yoda in the swamp to lift rocks. If you're not familiar with the movie already, watch the whole thing—although most junior highers are familiar with the *Star Wars* series, some students may not be, so be prepared to help students answer questions during this option.

> CAUTION
> At times, Yoda launches into some pretty strange monologues that conflict with a Christian worldview, so make sure you cue it to the right scene. Make it clear to students that you are not deriving biblical doctrine from the video.

Introduce the video clip with a brief summary of the characters and issues at hand. After the clip, discuss:

What was it that Luke wanted to learn? How to become a Jedi Master.

How did his training compare to his expectations? Luke doubted the wisdom and methods of Yoda who was trying to coach him. He couldn't see how lifting rocks fit into what he was trying to learn.

From this and other *Star Wars* movies, what do we know is the outcome of this training? Luke not only learned what he had hoped to learn, but he learned other important lessons like patience, self-control and trust.

Would Luke have learned his lessons without the help of Yoda? Probably not, because he needed Yoda's wisdom, insight and encouragement to learn and grow.

NOTES

Option 3 Tough Questions

You'll need The truth and nothing but the truth!

1. **If Jesus was God, why did He need help to grow?** According to Philippians 2:5-11, Jesus, although he was God, could at any time have used His privileges as God. Yet He laid aside those privileges and "emptied himself" as a slave to God. According to Hebrews 2:14-18 and 4:15, Jesus completely became flesh and blood, meaning He went through everything that we do as humans—yet without sin. Hebrews 5:8 says Jesus "learned obedience." In other words, although Jesus was God, He was also fully man.

2. **Why do I need to grow spiritually?** We need to grow spiritually because God created us as growing people. Just as we would be concerned about a teenager who still wore diapers and sucked on a pacifier, we need to be concerned if we are not growing spiritually. 1 Peter 2:2 teaches: "Like newborn infants, long for the pure, spiritual milk, so that by it you may grow into salvation" *(NRSV)*. We all need to begin with spiritual milk, but God wants us to grow up.

3. **If Christianity is a personal relationship with Jesus, why do I need other people to help me grow?** Our relationship with God through Jesus and the Holy Spirit is certainly the center of our faith; however, God desires and requires us to be in relationship with other Christians. As individual Christians we are all part of the Church that is compared to a family (see Romans 8:15-17), a living temple (see 1 Corinthians 3:16,17; 6:19,20) and a human body (see 1 Corinthians 12:12-27). Each of these metaphors captures the importance of having healthy relationships with other believers. There is no such thing as a Lone Ranger Christian.

4. **What do I do if I can't find someone who is perfect and can help me?** If you find a perfect spiritual helper, please send him my name and tell him I'd like to spend some time with him. Our spiritual coaches will often be people who have been Christians for longer

than we have, but sometimes God will even use new Christians to teach us valuable lessons.

5. **I'm only in junior high. Why can't I wait until I'm older to work on growing spiritually?** Being in junior high is the *best* time to begin the habit of seeking spiritual helpers. Believe it or not, the habits we develop in junior high will be some of the longest-lasting habits of our lives. So along with eating right, flossing our teeth and exercising, we need to get in the habit of finding spiritual coaches.

STEP
MOVING OUT

This step challenges students to actively seek help from others for spiritual growth in the next few days.

Option 1 — Light the Fire

You'll need paper, pens or pencils and treats for next week (see note below).

Ahead of time, prepare a list of names and phone numbers of adults in the church who would be willing to be interviewed by students.

Distribute paper and pens or pencils and ask students to write down three genuine questions they have about Christianity. Let students know that spiritual growth is a reward in itself, but you'll also have prizes for everyone who returns a completed form. (Distribute the list of willing interview candidates to students who need a starting point.)

> **Note:** Make sure you have the treats ready for those students who return their handouts next week. Never underestimate the power of reward!

Optional: End the session a little early and allow time for students to ask you or other adult leaders some of their questions.

Close in prayer, thanking God for the people that He's put in our lives who have helped us already and for the people God will use in the future to help us grow spiritually.

Option 2 — Fired Up

You'll need Copies of "Spiritual Goals" (p. 77), pens or pencils and a stack of Trivial Pursuit cards that you don't mind parting with.

Hold up a Trivial Pursuit card. Read each of the questions and answers; then explain: **Often we know the answers to questions that don't matter, but what about the answers to questions that do matter? If we want to grow spiritually, we need to begin asking the important questions and making plans about how to get answers.**

Distribute "Spiritual Goals" and instruct students to choose the goal they want to focus on. Ask them to find others in the room who have chosen the same goal; then have each goal-group follow the directions on the handout for its goal. Assign each student an accountability partner who will call or e-mail him during the week to see how he's progressing toward the goal.

In closing, pass out a Trivial Pursuit card to each student and challenge them to put the cards in a prominent spot in their rooms as a reminder that their spiritual lives are more important than trivial pursuits. Close in prayer, thanking God for the spiritual helpers students have already had and for the helpers God will use in their futures.

NOTES

Option 3

Spread the Fire

You'll need Copies of "Adult Advice" (p. 78) and copies of a list of adults who are willing to talk with students about sharing their faith.

    Ahead of time, compile a list of mature adults who would be available to help students answer the questions on the handout. (Be sure to get their permission first!)

Distribute "Adult Advice" and the list of adult helpers and explain: **Helping our friends hear about Christ is an area where we could all probably use some help. This week I want you to try to find one adult—someone you already know or someone from this list—and ask him or her to answer the questions on the handout.**

Youth Leader Tip

Be sure that you ask about this the next time you meet. There is nothing more demoralizing for students than when they remember what you asked them to do, but you don't.

And unless your students are more mature and responsible than the average junior highers, you and your adult team may want to call them during the week to remind them.

NOTES

Cool Coach

Your name:

The name of someone who coached you in your spiritual life:

How did you get to know your coach? Did you just become friends or did one of you make an extra effort to build the friendship?

What did you learn from your coach? What lessons, skills, habits did your coach help you learn and develop? (For example: having a quiet time, prayer, sharing your faith, studying the Bible, etc.)

How did your coach help you? (For example: you went to camp together and you talked during the bus ride; you were in the same small group; you lived in the same neighborhood and talked when you saw each other.)

Spiritual Goals

Name: _____   Date: _____

Spiritual Goal Categories

Check one of the following:

❑   Bible Study
❑   Prayer
❑   Evangelism
❑   Community Service
❑   Holy Spirit

Specific questions, issues or goals

1.

2.

Two people who might be able to help

1.

2.

Target date for talking to helpers: _____

Accountability partner: _____

Adult Advice

1. What do you think are the three most important things to do when you're talking about Jesus with someone?

2. What are the two worst things to do when you're talking about Jesus with someone?

3. What Bible verses or passages have helped you understand how to share your faith, and why are these so significant for you?

Adult Advice

1. What do you think are the three most important things to do when you're talking about Jesus with someone?

2. What are the two worst things to do when you're talking about Jesus with someone?

3. What Bible verses or passages have helped you understand how to share your faith, and why are these so significant for you?

Devotions in Motion

WEEK FIVE: JESUS: THE STUDENT WHO SOUGHT WISDOM

DAY 1

QUICK QUESTIONS

Read Proverbs 15:2 and learn how a fool and a fountain are alike.

God Says

If you had a plant you wanted to grow healthy and strong, how would you care for it?

- ☐ Feed it a steady diet of root beer and bubble gum.
- ☐ Play soccer and basketball with it every day.
- ☐ Sing to it and read it bedtime stories.
- ☐ Carefully water and fertilize it and give it the sunlight it needs.

I Do

What kind of people are you hanging out with? Are they the type of people who will help you grow with God? Or do they make your relationship with God seem silly or pointless?

Are you seeking out other people who will help you become closer to God? Choose two people who can help you grow in your relationship with God and make the effort to have a good conversation with them about God this week.

FOLD HERE ---

DAY 4

FAST FACTS

Hey, learn how to succeed with Proverbs 15:22.

God Says

Tina was going to throw the best party ever. She invited everyone she knew. Some of her friends offered to help; but Tina said, "Oh no, I want to throw this party all alone. I can do it and it is going to be the best party ever."

Well, the night of the party came. The guests would be arriving any minute, but Tina was nowhere near ready. She'd forgotten the music, the decorations weren't ready, the cake was burned; and Tina had no one to help her whip the party back into shape. She really wished she had the help of her friends now.

I Do

Do you ask your friends for help or advice when you need it or do you try to do everything yourself? Do you think that God wants you to rely on your friends or do you think He wants you to impress them with how much you can do all by yourself?

Pick one friend you can ask to help you with something today, and then work together on it.

FAST FACTS

Try to find Ecclesiastes 4:9-12 with your eyes crossed. It'll give you a headache, I promise.

God Says

Which of these would be the hardest to break with your hands?

☐ A single sheet of newspaper **OR** ☐ A whole newspaper

☐ One piece of aluminum foil **OR** ☐ A whole roll scrunched up into a big ball

☐ A single strand of dental floss **OR** ☐ A rope made of dental floss

I Do.

God knows it is hard to be a Christian and He doesn't want you to be alone! He wants you to have deep friendships with other Christians that bring you even closer to Him. Pray that in the coming weeks and months your circle of friends will become as strong as rope.

FOLD HERE -

QUICK QUESTIONS

Dive into 1 Samuel 23:15-18 and see what can make you stronger.

God Says

Minnie and Ginny don't do everything together or talk on the phone together every day, but they know that when one of them is in trouble and needs a friend, the other one will be there. Like when Ginny found out her grandmother had cancer, Minnie prayed with Ginny and helped Ginny remember that God was with her, even when bad stuff was happening. And when Minnie's parents decided to get a divorce, Ginny was around to help Minnie remember how much God loved her and cared about what happened to her.

I Do.

Good friends who help you know God better and rely on Him more are rare and very special. What kind of friends do you have? Do they build you up or tear you down?

And what kind of a friend are you? What can you do today to be a better friend to someone?

SESSIONSIXSESSIONSIXSESSIONSIXSESSIONSIX

The Big Idea

God can do huge miracles when you offer yourself to Him.

Session Aims

In this session you will guide students to:

- Learn that God wants them to bless the world with their resources;
- Feel eager to use whatever they have for God's purposes, even if it does not seem like they have much to offer;
- Act by using their gifts and resources for God's purposes this week.

The Biggest Verse

"When they had all had enough to eat, he said to his disciples, 'Gather the pieces that are left over. Let nothing be wasted.' So they gathered them and filled twelve baskets with the pieces of the five barley loaves left over by those who had eaten." John 6:12,13

Other Important Verses

Genesis 1—2; Matthew 7:9-11; Luke 12:7; John 6:3-15; 14:12

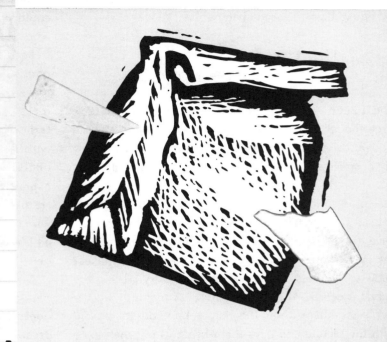

The Generous Kid Who Shared His Lunch

STEP
MOVING IN

This step helps students grasp that God loves to provide way more than they can imagine.

Option 1 Move It

You'll need A puzzle with 100 to 200 pieces and a table large enough to work the puzzle on. It would be best if each student has about eight pieces. If your group is particularly big or small, adjust the size of the puzzle accordingly.

Welcome students and distribute the puzzle pieces equally among them. Ask them to tell you what you just gave them. Hopefully the answer will be "Puzzle pieces!" Ask: **What picture do you think the puzzle makes?** Allow for guesses and invite students to try piecing the puzzle together. After a few minutes of trying to put the puzzle together without the picture, bring out the box lid with the picture and have them begin to put the puzzle together.

Explain: **Pieces of puzzles by themselves aren't much, but together they can be used to accomplish a lot. God can take every resource that we have and use them to make much more happen than we could ever imagine on our own. Today we're going to check out a guy who found this out firsthand.**

Option 2 Chat Room

You'll need Your Bible, a three-minute timer, paper and pens or pencils.

Welcome students and divide them into groups of three or four. Distribute a piece of paper and pens or pencils and explain that you are going to set the timer for two minutes and each group is going create a list of things students would like to have if money were no object. Groups should designate someone to write the list as everyone shares ideas.

After the time is up, invite groups to share their lists aloud; then discuss:

How might your lives change if your parents were able to give you everything you could ever want or need? Wouldn't have to worry about not having enough; would have confidence in our parents' ability to provide for us.

What would you say if I told you that you *do* have a parent who is able to give you even *more* than you could possibly imagine? (You should hear quite a bit of whooping and hollering!)

Read Ephesians 3:20 aloud; then explain: **As extravagant as some of our lists may be, God provides even more than we can ask for. What if I told you that the most awesome gifts He can give you never need batteries, gas, electricity or parts—because they come with an *eternal warranty*. He still gives us some of the material things we desire, but not even the most expensive item you can imagine can compare to what He has in store for us.** Read Romans 8:32 aloud: **"He who did not spare his own Son, but gave him up for us all—how will he not also, along with him, graciously give us all things?"**

God provides for *all* our needs—spiritual and material—abundantly. Read Psalm 23:5 and discuss: **So why doesn't He give us all the things on our wish lists?** Because He knows what's really best for us. He sees the whole picture. Continue: **Your six-month-old puppy sneaked a bite of your candy bar last week and now he drools every time he sees you eat chocolate. You know that chocolate isn't good for him; knowing more about him than he knows about himself, you are aware that chocolate is poisonous to dogs. All your puppy knows, though, is that you have the chocolate and that you're not giving it to him! He has to trust that you will provide what's best for him.**

Today we're going to meet a guy who found out firsthand what it means to trust that everything we need is provided abundantly by our heavenly Father.

Option 3 Fun and Games

You'll need An outdoor area or large indoor room.

Ahead of time, scope out an outdoor area or large indoor room for the activity and consider where you will designate boundaries for the game.

Greet students and explain: **The story we're going to check out today illustrates how Jesus used the sparsest** resources shared by one guy and provided for the needs of a multitude of people. Before we check out the story, though, we're going to play a game. Lead students to the room or outdoor area and point out the boundaries for the game. Select one person to be "It" and explain that you're going to play a tag game with a twist—every person caught by It must hold hands with It. Every time this happens, the additional person becomes part of It and joins in trying to tag people while continuing to hold hands with everyone who is It. Oh, we almost forgot one important rule: All players must stand or hop on one foot during the entire game! Anyone who falls is considered tagged and automatically becomes part of It. Begin the game and continue to play until everyone is part of the chain.

After the game has ended, transition to the next step by reminding students: **What started with one person in our game multiplied into something significantly greater. In the same way, God loves to take a little, multiply it and provide way more than we could imagine.**

STEP 2 — MOVING UP

This step teaches that God can use our resources to do miracles.

Option 1 — Move It

You'll need Supplies for banana splits—bananas, ice cream, whipped cream, toppings, bowls, spoons, a new rain gutter (approximately one foot of gutter for every four students), a table for the toppings and a large sheet or tarp to cover the whole table so that students won't see what is on it.

Ahead of time, set up the bowls, spoons and toppings for the banana split on a table and cover the table with something inconspicuous. Ask adult volunteers or parents to begin assembling the monster-size banana split by filling the rain gutter with bananas and ice cream in a separate room from where students will be. Arrange for a key word or phrase to let the volunteers know when to bring the monster banana split into the room.

Greet students and look a little embarrassed while you hold up one banana and a small bowl of ice cream. Explain that you had the intention of treating everyone to ice cream today, but evidently you didn't bring enough. Use the key word or phrase to cue the adults to bring the monster banana split into the room. Invite students to add their own toppings.

As students are enjoying their surprise, transition to the Bible story by explaining: **What happened today is just like what Jesus did with the small bit of lunch that a guy had brought with him.** Ask a volunteer to read John 6:3-15. Explain that while the young boy did not have much, he gave what he had and God multiplied it into something much greater. We never know what we might have that God might want to use to affect other people.

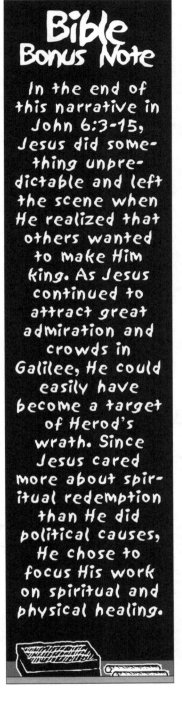

Bible Bonus Note

In the end of this narrative in John 6:3-15, Jesus did something unpredictable and left the scene when He realized that others wanted to make Him king. As Jesus continued to attract great admiration and crowds in Galilee, He could easily have become a target of Herod's wrath. Since Jesus cared more about spiritual redemption than He did political causes, He chose to focus His work on spiritual and physical healing.

The Generous Kid Who Shared His Lunch

Option 2  Chat Room

You'll need Several Bibles and some sports fan paraphernalia (a baseball cap, a pennant, a big foam hand, etc.).

Show students the sports fan paraphernalia and ask if any of them has ever been to a professional sports game (or local professional team) and ask: **What sport? Who did you see play? What do you remember about the experience?**

Read the following scenario:

Imagine that you're at a professional sports stadium filled with fans. You're getting hungry, so you decide to go to the concession stand to get something to eat. To your amazement, there's no line, so you are able to get your food right away.

You buy a couple of hot dogs, a bag of chips and a Coke and are happily making your way back to your seat when you hear the overhead announcement that there's no more food left in the entire stadium. Whew! You feel glad that you got your dinner just in time, yet as you look around, you realize that you are the only one who has any food.

Discuss: **How would you feel? Would you be willing to share? Why or why not?** Help students to be able to articulate reasons both for and against sharing (i.e., "It's good to share with others" or "My two hot dogs wouldn't really make a difference").

Explain that the Bible tells of a similar situation where there was a crowd of thousands of people who were hungry. Read John 6:3-15.

How would you have felt if you were the young boy and you had the only food available? Do you think you would have been willing to share? Why or why not?

After students have responded, conclude: **This guy was willing to share what he had. He didn't complain that it wasn't very much and certainly wasn't nearly enough to feed all those people; he didn't gripe to God that he was too young to be part of God's work. The boy gave what he had and God used it to miraculously feed *everyone*. That's not even the most amazing thing: Not only were all the people fed, but there were even lots of leftovers!**

Option 3  Pulse Points

You'll need Your Bible, a TV, a VCR, a blank videotape, a wig, a white board, a dry-erase marker and a tandem bicycle (or use the white board to draw one).

Ahead of time, videotape a local news program and cue the tape to a two- or three-minute clip spotlighting several needs around your community.

The Big Idea
God can use our resources to do miracles in providing for others.

The Big Question
What are the needs around us?

Introduce the discussion by playing the videotaped news clip; then explain: **When Jesus saw a need, He acted. Often He acted by using the people and resources around Him, as we see in John 6:3-15.** Read the passage and explain that there are three things noted in the passage that God wants us to know about the needs around us.

1. There is a need.
Explain: **That day around the Sea of Galilee, there were over 10,000 hungry people (5,000 men with at least another 5,000 women and children), and there was no 24-hour convenience store around the corner. That's a pretty big need. As a matter of fact, let's see how big that need is in terms we can understand.** Use the white board to illustrate as you explain following: **Assuming an average person would eat 1.5 McDonald's cheeseburgers (more for the men, fewer for the children) that translates to (1.5 x 10,000) 15,000 McDonald's cheeseburgers. Assuming you could even get the cheeseburgers on discount for $.39 per cheeseburger, that adds up to (15,000 x .39) $5,850. Add in fries and a Coke and you easily top $10,000 in catering expenses. Jesus knew there was a real need before Him. Fortunately, He also knew that God was eager to meet that need.**

2. God desires to meet that need.
Continue: **Because God cares about us, He cares about our needs. Sometimes we think God is only concerned**

with needs created by huge things like wars, famine and disease. He is concerned about those things and the needs they create, but He's also concerned about "smaller" things in our lives. For example, He didn't want the people listening to Jesus to go hungry—even for one meal. There's another place in the Bible in **Luke 12:7** where Jesus tells us about God's detailed knowledge of us and our needs. Put on the wig and read Luke 12:7. Continue: **I can put on this silly wig with all these zillions of hairs and God still knows how many hairs I have. In Matthew 7:9-11, Jesus describes God's perfect love by illustrating that as much as our worldly parents may love us and want to meet our needs, His love for us as His children and His desire to meet our needs is** *even greater.* Read Matthew 7:9-11 and explain that God is the perfect parent and *we* are His beloved children.

3. God invites us to join Him in meeting those needs.

Conclude: **While God is eager to meet the needs of the world, He is even more eager to involve us in His work. In the feeding of the thousands, Jesus allowed the boy to participate in God's miraculous work right beside Jesus' disciples. God wanted the boy and the disciples to be personally involved in the miracle so that their faith would grow and their love of God would deepen.**

Illustrate this by showing or drawing a tandem bicycle. Explain: **In many ways, working with God is like riding a tandem bicycle with Him in the front position steering and setting the pace. We are in the back position holding on and adding our pedal power. At times we may add a lot of energy to the pedaling and at other times it may seem like we're simply along for the ride. Either way, God enjoys our company and wants us to see the countryside as He sees it. It's amazing but true that God is eager to use us in His work in the world, changing lives and meeting real needs.**

STEP 3 — MOVING ON

This step reminds us that God can use the resources we have to bless others.

Option 1 — Chat Room

You'll need One copy of "Superhero Story" (p. 89) and a pen or pencil.

Ask students if they've ever filled out an ad-lib story, adding words where indicated (noun, verb, etc.), to create an interesting and surprising story. The key to these ad-lib stories is to fill out the missing words without reading the rest of the story so that when you're done, you'll be surprised by the story! To help students realize that God can use normal, everyday people to do amazing miracles, explain that together you're going to create an ad-lib story.

Read the descriptions of the missing words (i.e., name of student 1, number between one and six, etc.) and fill in the blanks using suggestions from the group. When you have filled in all the missing information, dramatically read the resulting story.

Transition by reminding students: **No one has to be a superhero to be used by God in super ways. We have a super God, so cooperating with Him allows us the opportunity to be involved in super miracles.** Invite students to share ways in which they have been used by God. Ask them to think of times when they prayed for people and saw their prayers answered or helped a person in need or shared the good news of God with their friends.

Option 2 — Real Life

You'll need Copies of "Baby-Sitting Money" (p. 90) and pens or pencils.

Ahead of time, cut the handouts apart.

> **Note:** What at first appears to be the same story on the handout is only the same at the beginning. Be sure to keep the top and bottom sections separated.

The Generous Kid Who Shared His Lunch

To make sure the stories don't get mixed up, give the copies of the top story to one volunteer and the copies of the bottom story to a different volunteer. Assign each volunteer a different side of the room and instruct them to wait to distribute the handouts until you give the OK.

Discuss: **How many of you like to baby-sit? What do you do with the money you make?** Divide students into groups of three or four and cue the volunteers to distribute the handouts as you explain: **Today we're going to check out a baby-sitter who decided to do something really cool with the money she made. One person in each group needs to read the story aloud and each group will have a few minutes to discuss the questions.**

After approximately seven minutes, bring students back into a large group and ask: **How many of you thought it was worth it to give the money so that the friend could go to camp? Why?** Pretty soon it should become apparent that students received different endings to the story.

Ask those who had the story where Dawn and her friend had a great experience: **Did any of you think that Dawn shouldn't have given the money to her friend? Why?**

Ask those who had the story where Dawn's friend was sick the whole time: **Did any of you think that Dawn shouldn't have given the money to her friend? Why?** If students don't make this point themselves, explain that even if we don't always see how our resources bless others, our job is to be faithful and offer them anyway. The boy in John 6 didn't know what would happen to his bread, but he offered and left what happened up to God.

Option 3 Tough Questions

You'll need Students with sharp minds to ponder these questions!

1. **Why does God need us to help Him?** God doesn't *need* us! He is all-powerful. He simply spoke all of creation into being (see Genesis 1—2). He can accomplish anything He chooses to do. However, in His desire for relationship, God has chosen to work with and through people. This is evident throughout the Bible from Genesis to Revelation with God using anyone from peasants to kings and everyone in between. He modeled His desire to work through humans in the form of His Son, Jesus, and He continues to work through us today.

2. **What if we don't have much to give?** The wonderful thing about working with God is that He is able to use whatever we have to do incredible things. God multiplies our contributions to meet the need. Sometimes the miracle is obvious, like when He fed thousands; sometimes it's subtle, like when people's lives are touched in ways we don't see.

3. **A friend who is really depressed about her mom's cancer comes to you and asks you, "Does God really do miracles today?" How would you answer?** Absolutely! However, our definitions and awareness of God's miracles may prevent us from recognizing them. For example, when we pray for someone to be healed of an illness and they get better after seeing a doctor, we might not attribute the healing to God and our prayers. One of the last things Jesus told His disciples was that they would do greater things than even He did. "Very truly, I tell you, the one who believes in me will also do the works that I do and, in fact, will do greater works than these, because I am going to the Father" (John 14:12, *NRSV*). Therefore, we should expect some mighty activity from God—and sometimes He will use *us* to carry out His miracles.

4. **If God provides so extravagantly and in such abundance, why don't I always have what I want?** The reason we don't get everything we want is due to one thing: sin. Our own sin alters our desires and makes them different from God's perfect will, which means that sometimes the things we desire would ultimately hurt us (or others). God withholds giving us some things we ask for because He sees the bigger picture and He knows what we need.

5. **What if we try to serve someone and nothing miraculous happens?** Well, we're not always going to be involved in such dramatic miracles as feeding thousands of people with a loaf of bread, but our job is to keep being faithful. As we are faithful, we can leave the results up to God, trusting Him to do what is best for us and others.

STEP 4

MOVING OUT

This step challenges students to be ready to offer their gifts and resources anytime God wants to use them for the purpose of blessing others.

Option 1 — Light the Fire

You'll need Copies of "Hands On" (p. 91), pens or pencils, a cassette tape recorder and a blank cassette.

Ahead of time, tape one minute each of five different kinds of music (such as classical, country, rock-and-roll, rap, jazz, etc.). Use a variety of styles to end up with approximately five minutes of music with distinctive differences.

Distribute "Hands On" and pens or pencils and explain that on the handout there are five different hands, each with a different phrase. Before you begin playing the cassette you made, instruct students to listen for the music style to change. Each time the style changes, students are to select a different hand and write down how they can relate what is written on the hand to what they have to offer God for His purpose. After playing the cassette, ask students to silently choose *one* thing they've written that they could do this week. Close in prayer, asking God to help students to be ready to give their resources to God this week for His purposes.

Option 2 — Fired Up

You'll need A white board and red, yellow, blue, green and brown dry-erase markers (or poster board and the same-colored felt-tip pens), enough snack-size bags of M&Ms for each student to have one, and one jumbo-size bag of M&Ms.

Brainstorm with students various gifts and resources that they as junior highers have to offer in blessing others and write down their ideas on the white board. Possible answers could include time, money, prayer, material possessions, etc. List their suggestions; then ask them to select what they think are the top five. Erase all but the top five and rewrite each of the remaining ideas in one of the following colors: red, yellow, blue, green and brown.

Pass the large bag of M&Ms around and ask each student to reach his or her hand in the bag and without looking take out one M&M, but do *not* eat it! Divide students into groups based on the color of the candy they selected and explain that their color M&M corresponds with one of the ideas on the list. Instruct the groups to discuss what it would look like for them to offer that particular resource to bless others.

Encourage them to share personal experiences where they have already shared this resource or where they have been the recipient of this resource. Ask them to imagine and share situations where they could see themselves offering that resource during the week ahead. Allow a few minutes of small-group discussion; then challenge students to look for opportunities in the week ahead to share that resource so that they can be part of God's work of blessing others. Close by having each group pray that they would see the opportunities God will put before them in the coming week and that they would be able to respond by offering their resources freely. Give each student a small bag of M&Ms as a reminder of the resource(s) they have to offer.

Option 3 — Spread the Fire

You'll need The same materials as the previous "Fired Up" Option 2.

Brainstorm with students various gifts and resources that they as junior highers have to offer in blessing others and write down their ideas on the white board. Possible answers could include time, money, prayer, material possessions, etc. List their suggestions; then ask them to select what they think are the top five. Erase all but the top five and rewrite each of the remaining ideas in one of the following colors: red, yellow, blue, green and brown.

Pass the large bag of M&Ms around and ask each student to reach his or her hand in the bag and without looking take out one M&M, but do *not* eat it! Divide students into groups based on the color of the candy they selected and explain that their color M&M corresponds with one of the ideas on the list. Instruct the groups to discuss what it would look like for them to offer that particular resource to bless others.

Regroup and ask for ideas for an outreach event that students could do together using all of their gifts (for example: a car wash, handing out cold sodas or water at the park, child care for a "Parent's Night Out," etc.).

Write the suggestions on the white board and discuss the different ideas. Work together to plan an event for students to participate in together. Let students know that you will check with church leaders to clarify the specifics during the next week and that you'll announce the details to students at next week's meeting. Close by reminding students that gifts aren't useful unless they're *used*!

NOTES

Superhero Story

A Day in the Life of Super-Christian

Having spent most of the night in prayer, (name of student 1) _____ rose at (number between one and six) _____ o'clock in order to memorize (a book of the Bible) _____ before heading to work as a (profession) _____. Breakfast consisted of (number) _____ (vegetable) _____s and a glass of (liquid) _____. Before becoming a Christian, (student 1) _____ enjoyed eating (animal) _____ but has since given it up since they are God's creatures, too. To protect the environment, (student 1) _____ (action verb) _____ to work instead of driving.

It only took (number) _____ minutes to get to work, since (student 1) _____ only came across (number) _____ broken down (plural noun) _____ with stranded owners. Once at the office, (student 1) _____ ran into (name of student 2) _____ who asked if she could (action verb) _____. "I'd love to a little later, (student 2) _____," said (student 1) _____, "but why don't you pull up a (noun) _____ and tell me what's on your (body part) _____." (student 2) _____ went on to explain that his/her (member of a family) _____ had just contracted (a disease) _____ and wanted (student 1) _____ to pray for (noun) _____. After a (number) _____ -minute-long prayer, (student 1) _____ closed with a (style of music) _____ hymn celebrating God's (adjective) _____ nature.

The rest of the workday was typical, with (number) _____ conversions during the (liquid) _____ break and (number) _____ conversions during lunch. On the way home, (student 1) _____ stopped by the shelter for (adjective) _____ (plural noun) _____ to offer a helping (body part) _____. Instead of eating dinner, (student 1) _____ sent it to (country) _____ where (student 1) _____ had read about (adjective) _____ (plural noun) _____ in need of (adjective) _____ food.

While getting ready for bed, (student 1) _____ flossed his/her (body part) _____ and prayed for (names of three students) _____, _____ and _____ who were having trouble (action verb) _____ in a Christ-like manner at school. (student 1) _____ then got down on his/her (plural body part) _____ and thanked God for the day's (adjective) _____ blessings.

Baby-Sitting Money

Dawn had baby-sitting jobs booked for five of the next six weekends. *This is great,* she thought, *I'll have enough money for a new stereo this summer for sure.* Although Dawn got pretty tired of baby-sitting and often wished she could just hang out with her friends on weekends, every time she would listen to her crummy little radio that only got AM stations, she would be more and more motivated to keep baby-sitting.

A week before she was going to go buy a new stereo, Dawn was getting a ride home from church from her friend Rebecca's mom. Rebecca and her mom were talking about camp, and Rebecca's mom told her she couldn't go because she was $100 short of the camp registration fee. Sitting there in silence in the back seat, Dawn couldn't help but think of the money that she had been saving for her stereo.

A few days later, Dawn decided to give Rebecca $100 from her stereo fund. It would mean she wouldn't get a stereo for a few months, but Dawn knew how much Rebecca wanted to go to camp.

Rebecca was so excited! All through camp, Rebecca kept thanking Dawn for the money. On the last night, the two prayed together that God would help them reach their campus and their friends. The two of them had never felt closer to God.

Do you think Dawn was right to give Rebecca the money to go to camp?

_____

If you were Dawn, what would you have done?

How do you think Dawn felt as she was driving home from camp on the church bus?

Baby-Sitting Money

Dawn had baby-sitting jobs booked for five of the next six weekends. *This is great,* she thought, *I'll have enough money for a new stereo this summer for sure.* Although Dawn got pretty tired of baby-sitting and often wished she could just hang out with her friends on weekends, every time she would listen to her crummy little radio that only got AM stations, she would be more and more motivated to keep baby-sitting.

A week before she was going to go buy a new stereo, Dawn was getting a ride home from church from her friend Rebecca's mom. Rebecca and her mom were talking about camp, and Rebecca's mom told her she couldn't go because she was $100 short of the camp registration fee. Sitting there in silence in the back seat, Dawn couldn't help but think of the money that she had been saving for her stereo.

A few days later, Dawn decided to give Rebecca $100 from her stereo fund. It would mean she wouldn't get a stereo for a few months, but Dawn knew how much Rebecca wanted to go to camp.

Rebecca was so excited! But then on the way up to camp, she ate something at a fast-food restaurant that made her so sick she spent the entire week at camp in her bunk (when she wasn't in the restroom vomiting!). Every time Dawn checked in on her, Rebecca would complain and say, "If only you hadn't given me the money, I wouldn't be here and feel so gross."

Do you think Dawn was right to give Rebecca the money to go to camp?

If you were Dawn, what would you have done?

How do you think Dawn felt as she was driving home from camp on the church bus?

Hands On

Write down your resources and the related gifts that you could use for God in blessing others. Use the following categories to help give you some ideas:

☞ **Time**
How can you use your free time to bless others rather than just seeking out what you want to do or what is fun?

☞ **Skills**
How could you help somebody this week?

☞ **Stuff**
(like your bike, CD player, etc.)
What stuff do you own that you might be able to loan to a friend?

☞ **Other Resources**
What other gifts and skills do you have that can bless others? (For example: a welcoming family environment, a pool for summer fun, new computer games, etc.)

☞ **Skills**
How could you help somebody this week?

☞ **Money**
How would you give some of your money to somebody in need?

Devotions in Motion

WEEK SIX: THE GENEROUS KID WHO SHARED HIS LUNCH

DAY 1

QUICK QUESTIONS

Flip to Acts 2:42-47. Is it garage-sale time?

God Says

If you had to choose one of these bags full of stuff to throw a party with, which one would you take?

☐ A small brown bag containing a half-eaten sandwich and an apple core

☐ A plastic grocery bag with a package of pens, some construction paper and a box of cookies inside

☐ A big black trash bag containing balloons, streamers and invitations

☐ A book full of cool party games and a beautiful bakery cake

I Do

What kind of things are you offering God to work with?

Are you just giving Him your leftovers or are you giving Him really cool stuff that He can do great things with?

What can you offer Him today?

FOLD HERE -

DAY 4

FAST FACTS

Hey, kiddo! Go and read 1 Peter 1:13-15.

God Says

Amy wasn't like the other kids at her school. When other girls spent their time gossiping on the phone after school, Amy volunteered to tutor math. When kids started to pick on a foreign exchange student, Amy invited the student to eat lunch with Amy and her friends. When it became cool to talk about what dorks parents and siblings were, Amy stayed quiet.

I Do

God wants us to be different, set apart from the people who don't know Him yet.

How do you behave? Are you like everyone else, except you go to church sometimes?

Or are you gentler, more giving and different from the crowd?

Today, how can you be different from people who don't know Jesus?

FAST FACTS

DAY 2

Read Luke 21:1-4 and see how *a little* to us is *a lot* to God.

God Says

Tom went to church every Sunday. His pastor was very fond of telling stories about missionaries and other people who did amazing things for Jesus such as standing in front of firing lines, giving away their last meal or helping captives escape from foreign prisons. Tom really wanted to serve God in an important way, but he just couldn't think of anything really big that he could do! "After all, there's no war or anything like that. There's nothing as important as that for me to do!" So he did nothing.

I Do.

Don't think for one second that God views what you do for Him as unimportant just because it doesn't make the front page of the local paper! God wants you to serve Him any way you can, even if it's "just" praying for other people or being obedient to your parents.

What kind of little things can you do for God?

FOLD HERE -

QUICK QUESTIONS

DAY 3

Stand on your head and read John 13:14-17 (OK, OK, you don't really have to stand on your head, but really do read John 13:14-17).

God Says

Imagine God coming up to you and asking you for the following things. What would you say?

"Okay, God, You can have it!"	**OR** "That's too much. I can't give You *that!*"
☐ The stuff in your trash can	☐
☐ Your dirty clothes	☐
☐ Your homework	☐
☐ Your favorite pair of shoes	☐
☐ Your candy stash	☐
☐ Your best sweater	☐
☐ Your bedroom	☐
☐ Your family	☐
☐ Yourself	☐

I Do.

What would you do if God asked you to give Him *all* of that stuff? Would you say, "Sure, no problem!"? Or would you ask if He could take it from someone else instead?

Ask God to help you be more willing to give Him anything He wants. You won't regret it. We promise. More importantly, God promises.

On the Move

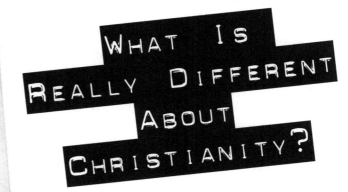

Maybe you've heard someone at school or one of your friends ask this question: "All religions are basically the same, right?" There's a one-word answer for that question: "No." This grid will help you see the differences between the key beliefs of four major world religions. See if you can figure out what makes Christianity so different from all other religions.

	Christianity	Judaism	Islam	Mormonism
What is the most important book?	*Holy Bible*—the 66 books of the Old and New Testament	*Torah*—the 39 books of the Hebrew Bible	*Koran* (also spelled *Quran*)	*Book of Mormon, Doctrine and Covenants, Pearl of Great Price* and the *King James Bible*
Who is Jesus?	God the Son, but also perfect man. The Messiah promised to the Jewish people, He was crucified for our sins, resurrected from the dead, ascended to heaven—Savior to all who believe in Him.	A Jewish radical who broke with tradition, but some do consider Him a prophet like Elijah or a prophet to the Gentiles.	One of many acknowledged prophets of Allah, but *not the* Son of God.	The Savior, but they believe He is a spirit who was created along with Satan and other angels. Many believe He married Martha and both Marys. Mary was literally impregnated by God (in human form) though she somehow remained a virgin.
Briefly describe God	God has always existed as three-in-one: Father, Son and Holy Spirit. He is holy, loving and just and He desires to be in relationship with us.	Yahweh who chose Israel as His people and promised to bless them so long as they worshiped Him alone and obeyed His Law.	Allah is the one god revealed most truly through Mohammed the prophet of Allah. All the world must submit to Allah and Islamic law.	God the Father, an excellent, holy man has human flesh and began the human race. A widespread belief is that God is married to "our heavenly mother."

	Christianity	Judaism	Islam	Mormonism
What does this religion believe about an after-life?	Those who have accepted Jesus Christ as Savior and Lord will go to be with Him in heaven. Those who do not choose to follow Him will spend eternity in hell separated from God.	The dead sleep until the Messiah comes and resurrects them; then He gives rewards and punishments for what people have done. Some will enter the glorious World to Come; others will be excluded.	Muslims believe in the Great Judgment of heaven and hell. Muslims hope that it is Allah's will to save them because of their decision to follow him. Gaining heaven is a great achievement.	There is no eternal hell; but there are three heavens: one for those who reject the Gospel, one for good people who rejected the Mormon message or didn't live up to the church's requirements, and then finally godhood.
Key distinctives of the religion	Based on joyfully receiving God's grace through Christ and voluntarily obeying God's plan. Believe in and follow Jesus and be changed through the application of the Bible to life and the power of His Holy Spirit. Two Great Commandments: Love God with all your heart, soul, mind and strength; and love your neighbor as yourself. Due to Christian missions, the only world religion that is truly global.	The study of Torah is the center of life. Adherence to the Ten Commandments and ethical (doing right things) monotheism (belief in one God only). The teachings of the Torah continue to be understood, interpreted and applied. The survival of the Jewish people through incredible hostility from many nations proves God's preserving power for His people.	It is an entire religious and political system that includes the Five Pillars (belief in the absolute oneness of Allah and his prophet Mohammed, prayer five times a day, required giving of money, fasting during Ramadan, and a pilgrimage to Mecca). Non-Muslims have fewer rights than Muslims, violence is used if non-Muslims protest.	People may evolve into gods if they believe the Mormon gospel, but they must also keep the laws of the Mormon church including baptism by immersion and doing good things. Non-Mormons who have led good lives must accept the Mormon gospel while in the interim spirit world after death and be baptized vicariously. The church keeps geneology records to assist Mormons who want "baptisms for the dead" performed for non-Mormon loved ones.

96

© 2000 by Gospel Light. Permission to photocopy granted. *Teens of the Bible*